ও।সা।১২৫

THE EDITOR, THE BLUENOSE
AND THE PROSTITUTE

On The "Hatrack"

From the Baltimore *Sun* of April 8, 1926.

the
EDITOR
the
BLUENOSE
and the
PROSTITUTE

H. L. Mencken's

HISTORY OF THE "HATRACK"
CENSORSHIP CASE

edited by Carl Bode

ROBERTS RINEHART, INC. PUBLISHERS

to Barbara with love

Published by Roberts Rinehart, Inc. Publishers, Post Office Box
3161, Boulder, Colorado 80303

International Standard Book Numbers 0-911797-40-8 (trade edition)
and 0-911797-48-3 (limited edition)
Library of Congress Catalog Card Number 87-92066
Printed in the United States of America
Typography, jacket, and binding design by Frederick R. Rinehart

First Printing March 1988

Contents

C · B
THE CONTEXT

BY CARL BODE

THE MAUL IS MIGHTIER THAN PATIENT REASONING

THE SACRED INSTITUTIONS

EX LIBRIS MENCKEN

MENCKEN

BIRTH CONTROL AN APOLOGY

ART OF SHOCKING THE FINER SENSIBILITIES

SCALPING THE YOKELS

EVOLUTION

APING GEORGE BERNARD PSHAW!

From the Memphis *Commercial Appeal* of April 6, 1926.

I

THE forces favoring censorship have always been for-
midable. They range from the programmatic to the
personal; from Plato's blueprint for the ideal state,
in his *Republic,* to the puritanical unconscious, if Mencken
can be believed, of the average American. In Mencken's private history of the "Hatrack" case, never before published,
we can see a prize example of a very aggressive censorship
and an illuminating example of how he battled to contain
it. We can also take a lesson from the case, for lessons evi-
dently are as necessary now as ever. The nightly news on
television and the reports in the daily papers testify to that.
A recent extension of censorship lies in the feminist assault
on pornography. Doubtless there are more extensions to
come.

Here we are going to be concerned with some of the major
ideas about and attitudes toward censorship, in other words,
the scaffolding surrounding the "Hatrack" controversy.

We might well start with Plato because he was probably
the possessor of the greatest of Western minds. Was he a
pioneer in the unceasing battle for free speech and

uninhibited writing? Far from it. He left no doubt about where he stood on censorship, and especially the censorship of literature. The most striking evidence comes in Book II of his *Republic*. There he has his spokesman, Socrates, discuss the education of the young and, by extension, the educating of persons of all ages. Socrates is talking to a pair of his disciples, Adeimantus and another man.

"The first thing," he announces, "will be to establish a censorship of the writers of fiction and let the censors receive any tale of fiction which is good, and reject the bad." Adeimantus asks what sort of tales would be considered good and who would write them? It turns out, as the discussion proceeds, that to Socrates all tales are basically bad because they all tell lies. He has no hesitation about naming the greatest of Greek authors as the most dangerous teller of lies: Homer. The more skillful the literary art, the more insidious the fabrications created. Though we may admire Homer we should never admire the products of his imagination.

What Adeimantus does not inquire about is who the censors would be. However, we can deduce from other parts of the *Republic* that they would come from the guardians of the young, who in turn would be picked by the philosopher-kings. After all, as Plato is careful to point out, he is describing the plan for a republic, not a democracy.

Socrates continues with his indictment in Book III. All poets, he warns, led by Homer, would do things harmful to the Republic. Poets are notorious for spreading slanders about the gods, even Zeus; and they spread lies about human beings as well. For instance, they assure us that "wicked men are often happy, and the good miserable; and that injustice is profitable when undetected." In Book X Socrates carries his criticism to its conclusion. Homer, even Homer, must be expelled from the ideal state because of his imaginings. Socrates does not give us the details since he has done that earlier when talking about the mime, who at that point represents all imaginative artists including poets. He is to be anointed with myrrh and crowned with a garland of wool but then driven into exile.

Plato found many like-minded successors. The nations of the West were ruled by a centuries-long sequence of monarchs, most of whom knew nothing about Plato but felt about censorship much as he did. In general, they censored for both moral and political reasons, just as he had proposed; and they shared his low view of the people.

The voices raised for freedom of expression were few, though here or there a major figure in our civilization managed to make his protest heard. In *Areopagitica,* issued in 1644, John Milton penned the classic argument for freedom of the press, yet even his devotion to it was not entire. While he robustly defended the right to publish without censorship, he conceded that the state had the right to condemn something after it was published.

Despite a handful of libertarians, censorship stayed alive and well. The Puritans, both in England and America, discounted Milton's argument, fellow Puritan though he was. When the infant colonies in New England were born, censorship sat comfortably by the cradle. Not infrequently a sermon or a tract, a treatise or a tome, was published but it was far from subversive. After all, the Puritans controlled the only printing press in New England, the one at Harvard College.

As time passed, Harvard itself produced intellectuals who defied censorship; yet they too were rare. Most of the waves of immigration that followed the founding of Massachusetts diluted the force of the original theocracy; on the other hand, the many immigrants from Ireland, particularly during the last half of the 19th century, followed the lead of their Catholic clergy in keeping a suspicious eye on the press. When censorship reached the yeasty 20th century it was not dismayed. As we shall see, it merely altered its manner of operation. Until 1926, when it collided with Mencken in his role as editor of the *American Mercury* magazine, it stayed the course.

II

The immediate cause of the collision was the attempt in Boston to stop the sale of the April issue on the ground that a vignette in it of a small-town prostitute nicknamed "Hatrack" was obscene. The sound of the collision reverberated throughout the country. Mencken played David against the Goliath of Puritan censorship with genuine skill. The truth was that he had been preparing to play the role for more than a decade. Early in his career he had decided that Puritanism was his arch-foe and censorship its most detestable expression. By the time he reached his mid-30s he could assure the controversial novelist Theodore Dreiser, "My whole life, once I get free from my present engagements, will be devoted to combatting Puritanism." He personified it in the form of a dour New England elder with pinched features, a blue nose, and frost in his bones.

Mencken examined contemporary Puritanism with the care and relish of a fighter training to destroy his opponent. The process brought a gleam to Mencken's eye and a ferocious grin to his lips. His definition of Puritanism was comprehensive indeed. In his most famous formulation he called it, grandly, "the haunting fear that someone, somewhere, may be happy." And he emblemized it in "The Kill-joy as a Moses."

On the other hand, when Mencken applied his mind as well as his emotions to the matter of Puritanism, he became more restrictive and more realistic. He recognized that the "witch-burners and the infant-damners" had gone to their reward. The old Puritanism had been eroded not only by immigration but also by the forces, more native than foreign, of liberalism and learning. Its remnant had largely left New England.

But Mencken was not alone in seeing that the urge to censor, the need to be one's brother's keeper, survived. The new Puritanism focused on morality as a matter of good taste and public order rather than as the operation of a Christian struggle against man's bent toward evil. Its hallmark became propriety rather than piety, and it transformed itself into an aspect of Victorianism. Its leadership was provided by the Boston aristocrats who were dubbed "The Brahmins" by critical observers. By the time of the "Hatrack" case the spirit of the old Puritanism, as Mencken himself remarked, had moved from New England to the Methodist prairies of the Midwest and the Baptist backwaters of the South.

The new Puritanism found its natural home in Boston, though it also emerged in New York and prospered there. In Boston the Cabots and their kind fashioned an agency for censorship in particular and public morals in general that, up to the fateful year 1926, proved to be perfect for its purposes. It was the New England Watch and Ward Society. While its officers came from the New England elite, its foot-soldiers came from the Boston Irish. Deep down, what united the two disparate groups was their chill hostility toward the pleasures of sex—and sex during the opening decades of the twentieth century was the time's most sensitive issue. The Brahmins and the Boston Irish found a highly effective agent in the Reverend Jason Franklin Chase, who in 1907 became the secretary of the Watch and Ward Society and soon thereafter its censor supreme. Though he tried to keep a low profile, he inevitably became the Society's spokesman as well.

His most notable speech stemmed from the "Hatrack" affair. He defiantly entitled the speech "The New Puritanism" and made it a manifesto. The plunge from Plato and his *Republic* to Chase and the manifesto is awesome. Yet, vast though the distance is, literally and figuratively, from ancient Athens to Boston of the 1920s, the two documents share their principal presuppositions.

Before we turn to the manifesto, however, we ought to examine one salient intervening document between Plato's and Chase's. Chronologically it is far closer to Chase's, for it came from Mencken's busy, battered typewriter. His essay "Puritanism as a Literary Force" appeared in 1917 as part of his *A Book of Prefaces.*

Although Mencken was no Plato and, thankfully, no Chase, his brilliant, combative essay has become a classic indictment of Puritan censorship. What afforded it added strength and renown during his lifetime was the fact that he buttressed it with his personal actions. These started with his aid to Dreiser in battling the censors, peaked in the "Hatrack" case, and continued till his disabling stroke in 1948. Though he had too much of a sense of humor to play the hero, he was ready enough to lay his body on the line, as we say nowadays, when he thought it really mattered. That was why he was willing to risk a prison sentence if he lost the "Hatrack" case.

"Puritanism as a Literary Force" was built on a pair of prior essays, both of which were part of a series on "The American." He published the series in the *Smart Set,* a raffish New York monthly whose literary critic he became in 1908 and whose co-editor he became in 1914. One essay dealt broadly with the morals of the American, especially the American male, while the other focused on the American as a New Puritan. Mencken came to the composition of these preliminary pieces, along with the final one in *A Book of Prefaces,* through years of exasperating experience. Much of the experience centered around Dreiser and the implacable realism of his novels.

III

From the time Mencken read Dreiser's first novel, *Sister Carrie,* printed in 1900 after much argument by his publisher, he knew that this was the novelist he was awaiting. After all, it was accepted in Puritan circles that the wages of sin were death. Here, however, was the story of a young woman who became the mistress first of one man and then of another. At the end of the book Carrie's second lover has killed himself; and Carrie, though saddened by her misadventures, is nevertheless a stage star. Life, to Dreiser, was like that.

Mencken and Dreiser were corresponding by August 1907, when Dreiser was a magazine editor and Mencken a beginning author. Although their friendship was to have its ups and downs, mutual professional respect always held it together. Then and later, the forces of censorship focused on Dreiser. And, as Mencken wrote Dreiser, the Puritans held almost all the cards. When Puritanism as censorship did not affect authors directly, it affected them indirectly. The most notorious censors were laymen with legal or quasi-legal connections. There were enough statutes on the law books about indecent literature to pose a constant threat.

In addition, various ultra-moral organizations made their appearance on the American scene during the late 19th and early 20th centuries. The most potent regional one was without doubt the Watch and Ward Society. The most potent national one, though headquartered in New York, made it its business to keep all of America clean. It was the Society for the Suppression of Vice, whose crusty leader was Anthony Comstock. Thanks to his zeal, plus all the legal sanctions he could invoke, he could boast near the end of his long life that he had brought 3600 people to court and had caused the destruction of 50 tons of books. He was equally zealous with magazines, for smut could rear its head in magazines as well as books. On magazines Comstock had a club that he never hesitated to wield. It was the Post Office regulation that if a periodical was twice judged to print indecencies, its 2nd-class mailing privilege could be revoked. If this happened it would mean the death of any commercial periodical. So Comstock had himself appointed, cosily, as a special agent for the Post Office. And that in almost all cases was that: a suspect journal seldom had a chance.

It was only with sweat and struggle that Dreiser continued to publish his novels. The one that the Puritans ultimately found the most offensive he entitled *The "Genius."* Its hero is a free-living artist. Because Dreiser had grown notorious for trying to bed every attractive woman who drew near him, the novel was patently autobiographical. Mencken was by no means unrealistic, so he warned Dreiser about what the censors would try to do to the book. In New York they denounced it for both blasphemy and obscenity. Mencken advised compromise until he discovered what the censors there—now captained by John Sumner, Comstock's successor—were demanding. They wanted to cut out 74 scenes of "lewdness" (mostly hugging and kissing), a short discourse on the female breast, and eight oaths such as "God damn!" and "Jesus Christ!" Mencken was incensed.

Doing his best to rally the literary community, he led the crusade to keep the censors from maiming Dreiser's book. He directed his abundant energies to circulating petitions, persuading the Authors' League of America to support Dreiser's cause, and at one point writing 20 or 30 letters a day for the sake of that cause. Unfortunately he got little help from Dreiser despite Dreiser's good intentions. "The old ass is ruining his case by his folly," Mencken complained to a friend. The most annoying reason was that, after Mencken had persuaded the conservative leaders of the Authors' League to endorse the protest and sign their names to the petition on Dreiser's behalf, Dreiser added the names of half a dozen Marxist nobodies from Greenwich Village, where he was living. Nevertheless, Mencken's efforts stalled the censors.

The correspondence, chiefly about the *Genius* affair, passing between Mencken and Dreiser in 1916—just ten years before "Hatrack"—highlights the experiences that intensified Mencken's animosity toward Puritanism. Those were the experiences that shaped the composition of "Puritanism as a Literary Force." From them he learned two things in particular. One was how trifling and silly the objections of the censors could be. The other was how influential the censors were because they had the support of their countrymen. Scratch any American, he wrote to Dreiser, "and you will find a Puritan," a Bluenose.

All the more reason then, Mencken realized, that he should prepare thoroughly for his frontal attack on Puritanism in its role as censor. He did not begrudge the time and effort the attack would take. His mode of composition helped. Unchanging throughout his career, it lent itself to the gradual development of his views on any topic important to him, prime among them Puritanism.

IV

Because he was a journalist Mencken was luckier than most authors, though he was also more ingenious and more energetic. His job at the *Baltimore Sunpapers* let him try his favorite ideas in the form of newspaper columns first. Then he usually expanded them into essays which he could print in magazines. He had an unlimited opportunity to display them in the *Smart Set* but he did not need to take much advantage of that fact. He soon made a name for himself as a lively and controversial essayist so that other magazines, not least the respected *Atlantic Monthly,* opened their pages to him. After periodical publication he put the final version of his views into book form.

A model instance was his three-stage preparation for producing *The American Language,* from "The Two Englishes" in the morning *Sun's* thriving offshoot, the *Evening Sun,* which became his permanent paper, for October 10, 1910, to "The American: His Language" in the *Smart Set* for August 1913, to *The American Language,* issued as a book in 1919 by the firm of his friend Alfred Knopf.

In developing his opinions for "Puritanism as a Literary Force" he worked along two complementary lines, both of which passed through the usual three stages. One line was to defend and promote Dreiser's ruthlessly realistic fiction. Sometimes he did this with columns he simply headed "Theodore Dreiser" or "Dreiseriana." At other times he picked more general titles but the pieces still featured Dreiser. A case in point: he wrote such a newspaper column as "The Novel Today" in the *Evening Sun* for March 22, 1911. Then he prepared such an essay as "Adventures among New Novels" for the *Smart Set* for August 1914; and lastly he expanded it into the 80-page appreciation "Theodore Dreiser" in *A Book of Prefaces.*

The other line was to attack Puritanism in general and the Puritan as censor in particular. On November 18, 1910 he wrote, for example, in the *Evening Sun* about "The Moral Mind." On October 25, 1915 he wrote a piece for the same paper headed "Notes for a Proposed Treatise upon the Origin and Nature of Puritanism"; on November 2 he published "More Notes" and returned twice to the topic during the next year. In between he composed the columns on Dreiser and his fiction. At the essay stage he printed the two solid contributions, mentioned earlier, to his "The American" series in the *Smart Set.* "The American: His Morals" came out in the July 1913 number. There he charged that the morals of the American people were deplorable because molded by democracy and that democracy was itself immoral since it substituted head-counts for principles. But the ire of the democratic majority about the minority resulted, he wrote, from something else: the continuing taint of Puritanism in the American character.

"The American: His New Puritanism" came out, with Mencken's accumulated evidence to support his charges, in February 1914. In it he showed that he believed in the ancient maxim, know your enemy. He had continued his homework, with the result that he exhibited a substantial if distorted knowledge of the history of American Puritanism, plus a first-hand acquaintance with its latest manifestations. He reiterated his thesis that the old Puritanism had dwelt on scouring away our own sins, while the new crusaded against the sins of others. As he phrased it there, the hairshirt was being replaced by the flaming sword.

To help in making every American behave, the New Puritanism had already created a variety of moral organizations. Mencken picked out, of course, as the two busiest and most belligerent the Watch and Ward Society and the Society for the Suppression of Vice. They were complemented by such purified and purifying societies as the YMCA. The "Y" marched to the melody of "Onward, Christian Soldiers." Along with its muscular Christianity went a zest for subjugating sin.

Against those perverse Americans who refused to conform to the ethics of the majority, the New Puritanism labored to enlist the forces of the law. The intention was to attack immorality with the weapons previously reserved for crime. Mencken picked the Postal Act of 1873 as the starting point for Puritanism's legal crusade against licentious literature and lustful arts.

However, in this full blown essay Mencken described the general advance of the New Puritanism, with only a mention of the efforts to censor literature. This did not mean that censorship was far from his thoughts. But it was not till 1917 that "Puritanism as a Literary Force" appeared in the *Prefaces* book along with, in nice compatibility, the long Dreiser essay. It proved to be well worth waiting for. It was a mordant attack, mounted with all Mencken's wit and vitality, on the New Puritanism as the premier policeman of American literature.

V

It remains a unique document in its magisterial mix of scorn and sociology. After Milton's *Areopagitica* it had no celebrated predecessors. Mencken put it this way: "I have gone into the anatomy and physiology of militant Puritanism because, so far as I know, the inquiry has not been attempted before." Nor, we can add, has it been attempted since, with anything like Mencken's drive. Here are its highpoints:

Mencken begins by accusing Puritanism of robbing American literature of its passion and beauty and of substituting a literature of right and wrong. For him the moralism of the average American is fortified by the moralism of the so-called literary critics. Even American humor is moral, proud though we are of it. Our greatest humorist, Mark Twain, the author of the matchless *Huckleberry Finn*, has been constrained to play the clown in public rather than the critic of life. It is America's fault that his genius has never been allowed to bloom fully.

During the final quarter of the 19th century, according to Mencken, there was some hope because of the emergence of a trio of diverse but highly gifted authors, besides Mark Twain: Henry James, William Dean Howells, and Bret Harte. But all four became stultified, in their various ways, by the pervasiveness of Puritanism. Mark Twain felt forced into the past when he was not clowning. Bret Harte sank into being a teller of idle tales. Howells and James "quickly showed that timorousness and reticence which are the distinguishing marks of the Puritan, even in his most intellectual incarnations. The American scene that they depicted with such meticulous care was chiefly peopled with marionettes."

The most stifling censorship arises from public disapproval. It can intimidate the sturdiest writer—with Dreiser as a splendid exception. Mark Twain himself confessed that he "dreaded . . . the disapproval of the people around" him. Besides the internalized Puritanism of the American public there is the external Puritanism which shows itself in laws and regulations—and which naturally includes an odious censorship. Mencken remarks on the relatively recent emergence of the professional purifier, the "moral expert," the man who decides when a novel or a play or a painting imperils public virtue. The purifier is often drafted as an expert witness when censorship cases get to court. His role models are New York's Comstock, Comstock's successor Sumner, and Chase, the high priest of censorship in New England. Like his models he is tireless in his labors for the Lord. Typically, he begins by barring John Cleland's *Fanny Hill* and ends by suppressing Zola and Balzac and Hardy.

The influence of the professional reformer on the legal process has been daunting. Mencken describes it in this essay with scholarly thoroughness, citing case after case of prosecutions under existing censorship statutes. Comstock and his descendants have waged a war of extermination "upon all ideas that [have] violated their private notions of virtue and decorum."

Up to this point Mencken is talking about censorship as suffered by authors and critics. Next he turns to the effect of censorship on the editors of magazines and on book publishers. He notes that he has paid his dues. Drawing on personal experience, he describes what happened when he co-edited the *Smart Set.* Although the magazine, despite its raffishness, was addressed to sophisticated readers, he found that he spent far more time in avoiding the reformers than in pleasing the magazine's patrons. His first question, he says, on looking at a submitted manuscript was, Would it pass the censors?

He explains how vulnerable a magazine is. "Any professional moralist [can] go before a police magistrate, get a warrant upon a simple affidavit, raid the office of the offending editor, seize all the magazines in sight, and keep them impounded until after the disposition of the case. Editors cannot afford to take this risk. Magazines are perishable goods. Even if, after a trial has been had, they are returned, they are worthless save as waste paper." Mencken ends his essay in indignation as he contemplates the damage to American literature inflicted by the moralists.

Here in the "Literary Force" essay he formulated his permanent position. He was libertarian, but his libertarianism was bounded by the constraints of reality and the dictates in sexual matters of bourgeois good taste. While he remained ready to take risks for freedom of speech, he also remained wary; for he never underestimated the censors. But their power made him all the hungrier to strike them a blow that would not only disable but humiliate. In effect, he was waiting for a "Hatrack" case.

Throughout the period that culminated in Mencken's publishing "Literary Force," the New Puritanism went its unmerry way, stopping the publication, it seemed, of almost anything it believed to be lascivious. After Mencken and Dreiser had emerged with a victory, if a ragged one, in the case of The "*Genius,*" we would anticipate that censorship would ease off. It did not. The censors rallied and were able to add the appeal of patriotism to their armament. After the United States entered the first World War in 1917, it became patriotic to be pure—at least in literature and the arts if not in private life. Mencken and Dreiser suffered as much from being stigmatized as unpatriotic as did any American literary figures. Both men bore German names; both men had been openly anti-British and pro-German before the United States entered the war. The result was that they were termed traitors by the most hostile members of the literary establishment, and their books were belabored because of their authors' lack of patriotism.

VI

After the war a backlash took place and Mencken, as a notably dissident intellectual, benefited richly, much more than Dreiser in fact. However, this by no means meant that the censors became idle; they still kept busy searching out sin on the printed page. Although we remember the decade of the 1920s as the era of the flapper and the hip flask, it was also the era when censorship was at its peak; the Blue-nose was busy indeed. In New England one important reason was Chase's strategy. He had devised a censorship system which was all the more effective because it was quiet. Under his walrus moustache he was alleged to have worn a perpetual scowl, but he had every right to make it a satisfied smirk.

The system operated out of his office in Boston. Mencken more than once described the process in irate admiration. What Chase had done was to promote the organization of a pair of self-censoring bodies. One was the Boston Booksellers' Committee; the other, the Massachusetts Magazine Committee. Whenever a book incurred his displeasure— and many did, including most of the novels by Dreiser along with such fiction as Sherwood Anderson's *Many Marriages* and Aldous Huxley's *Antic Hay*—he addressed an apparently low-key letter to the head of the booksellers' group, in the 1920s Richard Fuller, a Boston bookstore proprietor. He in turn warned the booksellers that Chase believed the book to contain passages that would be "held by our courts to be in violation of the statutes." At times a bookstore would defy Chase by selling the book but, as Mencken noted, Chase apparently did not lose one case in a hundred. The magazine committee, which represented the wholesalers and chain-retailers in the state, received the same quiet threat when some magazine contained material that made Chase glare. He would warn the chairman of the magazine committee, a Boston Irishman named John J. Tracey, and Tracey would pass on the word. Again Chase's record of successes was remarkable.

Throughout his years of triumph he ignored Mencken's books. We can only guess why he left them alone, but one reason was probably that they lacked any patent prurience. Such titles as *A Book of Prefaces* or *The American Language* or even *Prejudices: Third Series* failed to quicken his breath. When it came to magazines he probably ignored the *Smart Set* as being beneath his notice. Besides, Mencken was merely its co-editor.

The *American Mercury* was something else; it was a threat to the New Puritanism from the outset. Mencken did the major planning for the prospective magazine. His publisher, Knopf, helped; but the nominal co-editor, drama critic George Jean Nathan, had little sympathy for their aims. He wanted an up-graded *Smart Set;* Mencken wanted a vehicle for his ever growing interest in social criticism. A prospectus in the shape of a press release in August 1923 outlined Mencken's plans. The most significant sentences explained: "The aim of *The American Mercury* will be to offer a comprehensive picture, critically presented, of the entire American scene. It will not confine itself to the fine arts; in addition, there will be constant consideration of American politics, . . . American industrial and social relations, and American science. The point of view . . . will be that of the civilized minority."

These were no empty assurances. Mencken proceeded to bend every effort to make the magazine precisely what he had promised. Shortly after its first number, dated January 1924, he was able to take full editorial control. Now he had the weapon for social criticism that he yearned for. Puritanism was still at the top of his list, and he hoped to hit it on every level. To him its base was the element of Puritanism in the average American. Above that base came organized religion and especially the fundamentalist denominations. Though he conceded that the Irish Catholics were plainly inclined to Puritanism, he concentrated on the Methodists and the Baptists. Above them came the censorship organizations such as, inevitably, the Society for the Suppression of Vice and the Watch and Ward Society. Above all those stood the leaders of the two societies, John Sumner and Frank Chase.

As early as the March 1924 issue Mencken inaugurated his campaign, with satire and denigration as his favorite modes. He began with religion in general; for in the March issue he printed a piece by Arthur Ficke, a novelist and poet, called "Reflections of a Bible-Reader." Its conclusion was that "the reading of the Bible should be quietly discouraged." By February 1925 Mencken was becoming more specific; in the issue of that date he printed an acid bit of autobiography, "Up from Methodism," by the New York journalist Herbert Asbury. Gradually Mencken drew closer to his specific quarry, Chase. Because Mencken was a strong-minded editor he continued the practice started in the *Smart Set* of commissioning articles, if he did not have suitable ones already, on subjects that interested him. He failed to unearth a Boston reporter or writer willing to take on Chase. Since there did not seem to be any unChristian martyr in the

Boston area, Mencken had to go as far as Springfield, where he recruited one A. S. L. Wood, a book reviewer for the *Springfield Union*.

Wood's article appeared in the September 1925 issue under the title "Keeping the Puritans Pure." Though it sounded general it was actually a profile of Chase that ridiculed him from the first paragraph to the last. The centerpiece was an interview with Chase that he had rashly given Wood. Wood termed Chase "a reformer who would live up to the best tradition of the unctuous meddler." Although the piece contained a fair amount of biographical data, no one could accuse Wood of being objective. One of Mencken's informants in Boston reported that Chase was enraged. He was threatening to have the *Mercury* banned not only in Massachusetts but throughout the country. Delighted at drawing blood, Mencken had his assistant, an ex-Bostonian named Charles Angoff, prepare a scurrilous article on the sad state of the Bostonian mind. "Boston Twilight" appeared in the December 1925 issue. Though it went beyond Chase and dealt broadly with this renaissance in reverse, it noted his part in bringing about the twilight.

In the April 1926 issue Mencken redoubled his efforts, literally, for he ran two articles calculated to irritate Chase. The first, entitled "The Methodists," was written by Angoff under a pseudonym. More temperate and more factual than "Boston Twilight," it described the southern, fundamentalist branch of the Methodist church as it continued its rigid refusal to unite with the northern branch. The piece included a scornful paragraph about Chase as "a Methodist vice-hunter of long practice and great natural talent." The second article was "Hatrack."

The theme of "Hatrack" was Christian hypocrisy. Each Sunday night the prostitute nicknamed Hatrack attended church in her little Missouri town of Farmington, hoping to be treated as a fellow Christian. Each Sunday she was spurned, so after church she took her fellowship in one of the two town cemeteries. Gifted with her own kind of tact, she lay with her Protestant customers only in the Catholic cemetery and with her Catholic ones solely in the Masonic cemetery.

Enough was enough, and Chase moved to bar the April issue from the newsstands. On March 27 he mailed a copy of the customary notice to John Tracey, who notified the newsstand operators. It contained the customary threat of legal action. As usual also, Chase did not sign his name, writing instead as the Watch and Ward Society. However, he departed from his time-tested procedure in two risky respects. By issuing a statement to the Boston papers he let his role become public; and he specified "Hatrack" as the threat to New England morals. We can only guess that a combination of anger and arrogance made him reckless. In his statement he charged that "Hatrack" was immoral, unfit to read, and vicious; consequently, the April issue had to be outlawed.

While there is no need to tell the tale of the "Hatrack" case here when Mencken's own full-blown account is coming, it would probably be useful to sum it up in a paragraph:

Having decided to fight Chase and all he stood for, Mencken entrained for Boston, beguiled Chase into buying a copy of the banned issue, and got himself arrested. Promptly tried for selling improper literature, he was promptly acquitted by a judge who had taken the trouble to read the whole issue overnight and was impressed by its intellectual qualities. But, moving equally promptly, Chase went to New York, visited the federal Post Office there and prevailed on its officials to have Washington bar the issue from the mails. Mencken took both Watch and Ward and the Post Office to court. However, both institutions emerged with paper victories, for he finally dropped the case against Watch and Ward, and a federal judge ruled in favor of the Post Office. While neither institution came out unscarred, Mencken failed to win the legal victory that the nation's press—and doubtless the nation itself—believed he had. But he did win a moral one.

From the first day the case attracted national attention, for it had prime news value. Moreover, from the time the judge's decision was delivered it promised to become a bulwark for the freedom of the press. The multitude of newspaper clippings in the "Hatrack" scrap-books that Mencken kept testify to the fact.

A fortnight after the case broke, Chase did something else. He furnished us with the theoretical basis for the censorship that in more ways than one descended from Plato's. This he did through his highly rhetorical address, mentioned before, "The New Puritanism," which he delivered at Harvard's Student Liberal Club. Mencken secured the galleys from the Harvard *Advocate* for the scrap-books. As the *Advocate* observed, the address spoke not only for Chase but for the organization whose guiding spirit he long had been.

VII

The address gives every sign of having been drafted in haste as well as indignation and self-defense. But what the "Hatrack" case probably did was to crystallize opinions Chase had held for a generation. That his pivotal points are Platonic is partly disguised by differences in style and substance. The difference between Plato's lucid dialogues and Chase's overblown exhortations is of course great. So is the difference in auxiliary points, since one document is Grecian while the other is American. In the American one we find that Plato's views are diluted by democracy and distorted by the American emphasis on sex. Still, the address

is the outstanding statement by a Puritan about the New
Puritanism as evidenced in censorship. And the theoretical
basis for that censorship is still traditional.

Chase opens with a tribute to "the spiritual mother of
us all, old Puritan Massachusetts" but then piously admits
that the old Puritanism was not perfect. It was hard, aus-
tere, and unlovely. His new Puritanism, however, is dis-
tinguished by its loftiness and beauty. Righteousness is the
rock on which the Bay State rests; and the New Puritan
movement has three lofty objects to attain, three kinds of
righteousness: social, civic, and individual.

The aim of social righteousness is to make vice a crime
in the eyes of the law. The special target should be not so
much the evil individuals as the corrupting organizations
that pander to "lust, luck, and lethe"—in other words, to
immorality, gambling, and drugs.

Many good laws have been passed but they are not always
enforced. While the task of social righteousness is to see
that the proper laws are in place, the task of civic righteousness is to mobilize public opinion and so assist the police
and the courts. If this is not done, many a person young
or old will be lured by vice. "Obscenity is a short way to
the brothel, and the brothel is the entrance to Hell." In fact,
even our cafes are "the white slave marts of women's purity
and the slaughter houses of men's honor." Chase goes on
to inveigh against immoral literature, of the sort that New
York publishers are putting out in reams. The evil effect
of such literature can scarcely be overestimated. "A whole
High School Class of unwedded mothers may be the result
of a lascivious book."

Such literature cries to be censored, and the American
way of censorship is to enforce the law. However, Chase
says with pride, Boston has a set of high-minded booksellers
who regularly do their own censoring. He neglects to mention that in many instances the suggestion to censor origi-

nates in his office at Watch and Ward. Anyhow, the zeal for public morality has come from the old Puritans; and it has been preserved not only in the remaining descendants of the first settlers but in the aliens who have surged by now onto New England's shores. "The Boston of the Cabots, the Ameses, the Lowells, and the Lodges has not essentially changed in becoming the Boston of the Sullivans, the Fitzgeralds, the Galvins, and the Walshes."

The third aim is the revival of individual righteousness. Here Chase would find Mencken in agreement with his analysis. The sign of the Old Puritanism was the individual's concern with his own righteousness. He was personally responsible to God, as Chase phrases it. He had to attend to his own goodness before assisting in his neighbor's.

It is in the spirit of the New Puritanism that we must carry on, despite the existence of the "calumny and vilification into which a reform worker is often thrown in his attempt to fight Vice." Chase exhorts his young audience, in winding up his address, that we must fight "until our work is ended."

Until our work is ended . . .

For Chase its end came soon. He died in November, eight months after the "Hatrack" imbroglio began, and the members of Boston's moral establishment lamented his passing. But many other Bostonians obviously did not, though few attacked him from the outset with the waspishness of the editors of the *Boston Telegram.* Their headline of April 23 set the tone: "J. Frank Chase, Discredited and Shunned, Reported Ready to Quit Boston"; and it was reinforced by the lead in the story: "J. Frank Chase is 'all through' as a fake reformer."

Of the other characters in our drama, Mencken remained during the rest of the 1920s the country's key social critic. The pundit Walter Lippmann hailed him, a few weeks after Chase's death, as "the most powerful personal influence on this whole generation of educated people." But the Great Depression sent him into limbo. Though he continued to write colorfully on political issues, readers abandoned him in droves. When he started to reminisce about his Baltimore boyhood and his experiences as a rambunctious young reporter, however, he won many of them back. They delighted in the three volumes of mellow memories that he published. His stroke in 1948 cut off his career though he lived till 1956.

He never published his account of the "Hatrack" case. He composed it with remarkable care in 1937 and annotated it more fully than anything else he ever wrote. He could levy on enough documentation, chiefly newspaper clippings, to fill five of the ten large scrap-books. Yet the hope he had for the account was modest indeed considering the effort he expended on it: "It is conceivable that this detailed narrative of the 'Hatrack' case may some day interest an historian of American culture in the early Twentieth Century."

Perhaps he was modest because he realized that his narrative was uneven. The first third was enlivened by the presence of Chase, who served, from Mencken's point of view, as the perfect Puritan villain. However, he died inconveniently early, though Mencken's feud with Watch and Ward continued. The rest of the account was less lively because the only possible successor to Chase was merely a bigoted if powerful bureaucrat, one Horace Donnelly, Solicitor for the Post Office Department. Even Mencken failed to make the legal maneuverings he described in the last two-thirds of his account very interesting. He said in his Prefatory Note that the fully documented account would go to the New York Public Library, but he actually left it to the Enoch Pratt Free Library.

After "Hatrack" and "Up from Methodism" Herbert Asbury turned his journalistic talents more and more to freelance writing. Over the years he published a variety of books, all in a lively historical vein. Among them were: *The Gangs of New York, The Barbary Coast,* and *The Great Illusion, an Informal History of Prohibition.* Mencken no doubt approved. Asbury died in 1963.

And Hatrack herself? The scrap-books tell us that long before her rise to notoriety she had left Farmington, where Asbury had known her, and had moved to nearby Flat River. There, after her three children by a prior marriage were consigned to an orphan asylum, she married again. She soon faded from the pages of the newspapers and, we trust, lived happily ever after despite a few failings. At any rate, the prospects were good. The *San Francisco News*'s headline shortly after the case broke was: " 'Hatrack' is Found Happily Wed."

H·A

HATRACK

BY HERBERT ASBURY

W HEN I was a boy in Farmington, Missouri, it was the custom of our pastors and pious brethren, and of the professional devil-chasers who were imported as reinforcements from time to time, to proclaim loudly and incessantly that our collective morals were compounded of a slice of Sodom and a cut of Gomorrah, with an extract of Babylon to flavor the stew. They worried constantly and fretfully over our amorous activities; they regarded every man except the very aged and decrepit as a potential seducer, and every young girl as a prospective daughter of sin, whose salvation depended almost entirely upon the volume of noise they themselves could make.

In their more feverish discourses appeared significant references to the great difficulty of remaining pure, and in effect they advised our young women to go armed to the teeth, prepared to do battle in defense of their virginity. These gloomy predictions of the inevitability of seduction naturally had a tremendous effect upon young minds; very likely it was after she had heard the ravings of such an evangelist that the little girl of the fable, requested by her teacher to define a virgin, replied, "A female person under five years of age."

In all the small towns of the Middle West this sort of thing was the principal stock in trade of those who would lead their brethren to the worship of the current God. I do not recall ever having heard an evangelist, whether professional or amateur, who did not assure his hearers that their town was over-run by harlots, and that brothels abounded in which leading citizens abandoned themselves to shameful orgies while church attendance dwindled, and collections became smaller and smaller, and chicken appeared less and less frequently upon the ministerial table. Their tirades were generally in this fashion:

> Shall we permit these painted daughters of Jezebel, these bedizened hussies, to stalk the streets of this fair city and flaunt their sin in the face of the Lord? Shall we permit them to lure our sons and brothers into their vile haunts and ply their nefarious trade in the very shadow of the House of God? No! I say NO! Jesus Christ must live in this town!

Immediately everyone shouted, "Amen, Brother!" and "Praise the Lord!" But it was sometimes difficult to determine whether the congregation praised the Lord for inspiring the evangelist to so courageously defy the harlots, or for permitting him to discover them. If the Man of God could find them, why not the damned too? Certainly there were always many who wondered if the brother had acquired any good addresses or telephone numbers since coming to town. Not infrequently, indeed, he was stealthily shadowed home by young men eager to settle that question.

These charges and denunciations were repeated by the evangelist at the meetings for men only which were always a most interesting feature of the revivals. At similar gatherings for women, or ladies, as we called them in small town journalism, his wife or a devout sister discussed the question from the feminine viewpoint. What went on at these latter conclaves I do not know, though I can guess, for I have often seen young girls coming out of them giggling and blushing. The meetings for men only were juicy indeed. The evangelist discussed all angles of the subject, and in a very free manner. His own amorous exploits before he became converted were recited in considerable detail, and he painted vivid word pictures of the brothels he had visited, both as a paying client and in the course of his holy work. Almost invariably they were subterranean palaces hung with silks and satins, with soft rugs upon the floor, and filled with a vast multitude of handsome young women, all as loose as ashes. Having thus intimated, with some smirking, that for many years he was almost the sole support of harlotry, he became confidential. He leaned forward and said:

"There are such Dens of the Devil right here in your town!"

This was first-class information, and immediately there was a stir in the audience, many of his hearers betraying an eagerness to be gone. But before they could get away the evangelist thundered:

"Shall we permit them to continue their wicked practices?"

I always hoped to be present some day when the audience forgot itself and answered that question with the reply that was so plainly in its mind, namely, "Yes!" But alas, I never heard it, although there was much shouting of "Amen!" and "Glory to God!" These meetings for men only were generally held in the afternoon, and their net result was that the business of the drug-store increased immediately, and when night fell bands of young good-for-nothings scurried hither and yon about the town, searching feverishly for the Dens of the Devil. They searched without fear, confident that modern science would save them from any untoward consequences, and knowing that no matter what they did they would go to heaven if they permitted a minister to intercede for them in the end, or a priest to oil them with holy unguents.

But the Dens of the Devil were not found, neither in Farmington nor in any other small town in that region, for the very good reason that they did not exist. The evangelist did not know what he was talking about, he was simply using stock blather that he had found by experience would excite the weak-minded to both sexual and religious emotions, which are very similar. He knew that when they were thus upset they would be less likely to question his ravings—that they would be more pliable in his hands and easier to convert. It is, in fact, well-nigh impossible to convert anyone who can keep his head and retain control of his emotions. Such a person is likely to giggle during the most solemn moments, and nothing is more destructive of evangelical fervor than a hearty giggle.

II

Our small towns were not over-run by harlots for the plain reason that harlotry could not flourish in a small town. It was economically impossible; there were not enough cash customers to make the scarlet career profitable. Also, the poor girls had to meet too much competition from emotional ladies who had the professional spirit but retained their amateur standing by various technicalities. And harlots, like the rest of us, had to live; they required the same sort of raiment and food that sufficed their virtuous sisters; it was not until they died that they wore nothing but the smoke of hell and were able to subsist on a diet of brimstone and sulphur.

Many men who in larger communities would have patronized the professionals could not do so in a small town. They could not afford to; it was too dangerous. The moment a woman was suspected of being a harlot she was watched eagerly by everyone from the mayor down to the preachers, and the name of every man seen talking to her, or even looking at her, went winging swiftly from mouth to mouth, and was finally posted on the heavenly bulletin board as that of an immoral wretch. A house in which harlotry was practiced was picketed day and night by small boys eager to learn the forbidden mysteries, and by brethren and sisters hopefully sniffing. It was not possible for a harlot to keep her cliéntèle secret, for the sexual life of a small town is an open book, and news of amorous doings could not travel faster if each had a tabloid newspaper.

Exact statistics, of course, are not available, but it is probably true that no small American town has ever harbored a harlot whose professional income was sufficient to feed and clothe her. Few if any such towns have ever been the abode of more than one harlot at a time. When I was a boy every one had its own harlot, just as it had its town sot (this, of course, was before drunkards became extinct), and its town idiot. But she was generally a poor creature who was employed by day as a domestic servant and practised her ancient art only in her hours of leisure. She turned to it partly for economic reasons, and partly because of a great yearning for human companionship, which she could obtain in no other way. She remained in it because she was almost instantly branded a Daughter of Satan, and shunned by good and bad alike. She seldom, if ever, realized that she was doing wrong; her moral standards were those of a bed-bug. She thought of harlotry in terms of new ribbons and an occasional pair of shoes, and in terms of social intercourse; she was unmoral rather than immoral, and the proceeds of her profession, to her, were just so much extra spending money.

Small town men who occasionally visited the larger cities,

and there thought nothing of spending from ten to fifty dollars in metropolitan brothels, were very stingy in dealing with the town harlot. They considered a dollar an enormous price for her, and frequently they refused to give her anything. Many small communities were not able to support even a part-time harlot; consequently some members of the craft went from town to town, taking secular jobs and practicing harlotry as a side line until driven out by the godly or until the inevitable business depression occurred. I recall one who made several towns along the O.K. Railroad in Northeastern Missouri as regularly as the shoe drummers. Her studio was always an empty box car on the town siding, and she had a mania for inscribing in such cars the exact dates and hours of her adventures, and her honoraria. It was not unusual to find in a car some such inscription as this:

Ten p.m., July 8. Fifty cents.

These writings, scrawled in lead pencil or with a bit of chalk, were signed "Box Car Molly." Once, in a car from which I had unloaded many heavy bags of cement, I came across what seemed to be a choice bit of very early, and apparently authentic Box-Car-Molliana. On the wall was this:

I was ruined in this car May 10.

Box Car Molly

III

Our town harlot in Farmington was a scrawny creature called variously Fanny Fewclothes and Hatrack, but usually the latter in deference to her figure. When she stood with her arms outstretched she bore a remarkable resemblance to the tall hatracks then in general use in our homes, and since she was always most amiable and obliging, she was frequently asked to pose thus for the benefit of drummers and other infidels. In time, she came to take a considerable pride in this accomplishment; she referred to herself as a model, and talked vaguely of abandoning her wicked life and going to St. Louis, where she was sure she could make a living posing for artists.

Six days a week Hatrack was a competent and more or less virtuous drudge employed by one of our best families, but Sunday was her day off, and she then, in turn, offered her soul to the Lord and went to the devil. For the latter purpose she utilized the Masonic and Catholic cemeteries, which were side by side, although their occupants presumably went to different heavens. Hatrack's regular Sunday night parade, her descent from righteousness to sin, was one of the most fascinating events of the week, and promptly after supper those of us who did not have engagements to take young ladies to church (which was practically equivalent to publishing the banns), went downtown to the loafing place in front of the Post Office and waited impatiently.

On week days Hatrack turned a deaf ear to the blandishments of our roués, but on Sunday night she was very gracious and receptive. This, however, was not until she had gone to church and had been given to understand, tacitly but none the less clearly, that there was no room for her in the Kingdom of Heaven. Our Sunday night services usually began about eight o'clock, following the meetings of the various young people's societies. At seven thirty, regardless of the weather, the angular figure of Hatrack could be discerned coming down the hill from the direction of the cemeteries. She lived somewhere in that section and worked by the day. She was always dressed in her best, and in her eyes was the light of a great resolve. She was going to church, and there was that in her walk and manner which said that thereafter she was going to lead a better life.

There was always a group of men waiting for her around the Post Office. But although several always muttered, "Here she comes!" it was not good form to speak to her then, and she walked past them as though she had not seen them. But they, with their wide knowledge of the vagaries of the agents of the Lord, grinned hopefully and settled down to wait. They knew she would be back. She went on up the street past the Court House and turned into the Northern Methodist Church, where she took a seat in the last row. All about her were empty seats; if they were not empty when she got there they were soon vacated. No one spoke to her. No one asked her to come to Jesus. No one held out a welcoming hand. No one prayed for her. No one offered her a hymn-book. At the protracted meetings and revivals, which she invariably attended, none of the brothers and sisters tried to convert her; she was a Scarlet Woman and belonged to the devil. There was no place for her in a respectable congregation. They could not afford to be seen talking to her, even in church, where God's love, by their theory, made brothers and sisters of us all.

It was painful to watch her; she listened to the Word with such rapt attention; she sang the hymns with such fanatical fervor, and she plainly yearned for the comforts of that barbaric religion and the blessings of easy intercourse with decent people. But she never got them. From the Christians and their God she got nothing but scorn. Of all the sinners in our town Hatrack would have been the easiest to convert; she was so eager for salvation. If a preacher, or a brother, or a sister, had so much as spoken a kind word to her she would have dropped to her knees and given up her soul. And her conversion, in all likelihood, would have been permanent, for she was not mentally equipped for a struggle against the grandiose improbabilities of revealed religion. If someone had told her, as I was told, that God was an old man with long whiskers, she would not have called him "Daddy," as some of her more flippant city sisters might have done; she would have accepted Him and gloried in Him.

But she was not plucked from the burning, for the workers for the Lord would have nothing to do with her, and by the end of the service her eyes had grown sullen and her lip had curled upward in a sneer. Before the final hymn was sung and the benediction pronounced upon the congregation she got to her feet and left the church. None tried to stop her; she was not wanted in the House of God. I have seen her sit alone and miserably unhappy while the preacher bellowed a sermon about forgiveness, with the whole church rocking to a chorus of "amens" as he told the stories of various Biblical harlots, and how God had forgiven them.

But for Hatrack there was no forgiveness. Mary Magdalene was a Saint in heaven, but Hatrack remained a harlot in Farmington. Every Sunday night for years she went through the same procedure. She was hopeful always that someone would speak to her and make a place for her, that the brothers and sisters who talked so volubly about the grace and the mercy of God would offer her some of the religion that they dripped so freely over everyone else in town. But they did not, and so she went back down the street to the Post Office, swishing her skirts and offering herself to all who desired her. The men who had been waiting for her, and who had known that she would come, leered at her and hailed her with obscene speech and gesture. And she gave them back leer for leer, meeting their sallies with giggles, and motioning with her head toward the cemeteries.

And so she went up the hill. A little while later a man

left the group, remarking that he must go home. He followed her. And a moment after that another left, and then another, until behind Hatrack was a line of men, about one to a block, who would not look at one another, and who looked sheepishly at the ground when they met anyone coming the other way. As each man accosted her in turn Hatrack inquired whether he was a Protestant or a Catholic. If he was a Protestant she took him into the Catholic cemetery; if he was a Catholic they went into the Masonic cemetery. They paid her what they liked, or nothing, and she was grateful for whatever she received. It was Hatrack who made the remark that was famous in our town for many years. To a stranger who offered her a dollar she said:

"You know damned well I haven't got any change."

H·L·M
THE "HATRACK" CASE

THE AMERICAN MERCURY
VS.
THE NEW ENGLAND
WATCH AND WARD SOCIETY,
THE POSTMASTER-GENERAL
OF THE UNITED STATES,
ET AL.

BY H. L. MENCKEN

1937

PREFATORY NOTE*

THIS record is based upon my own notes and recollections, upon memoranda furnished by other participants, upon the letter files of the *American Mercury* and of the lawyers engaged in the case, upon the contemporary newspaper reports of it and comments upon it, and upon various other documents. The introductory narrative is reasonably complete, and, I believe, substantially accurate. All names, dates and other such references have been verified. During the progress of the case I made notes of all important transactions, conversations and observations,

---

*Textual note. In the pages that follow, Mencken's annotations are omitted; his fully annotated text can be found in the Enoch Pratt Free Library. There must have been at least two prior drafts of that text. In one, which he titled "Fair Copy . . . with Corrections, 1937," he penned many minor emendations. In it he also pasted numerous passages clipped from an earlier draft. His secretary incorporated the emendations and pasted-in passages in the text being published here. The "Fair Copy" contains an afterthought, dated 1947, saying that he has given the "Hatrack" papers to the Enoch Pratt Free Library instead of to the New York Public Library, as he had originally intended.

and these notes have been put to frequent use. The legal documents, of course, were easily accessible, and Arthur Garfield Hays, the chief counsel for the *American Mercury,* put at my disposal what remained of his correspondence with his Boston associate, Herbert B. Ehrmann, and with the counsel for the Watch and Ward Society and the Postoffice. Others to whom I am indebted for material are Herbert Asbury, the author of "Hatrack"; Alfred A. Knopf, publisher of the *American Mercury* from 1924 to 1935; Lawrence E. Spivak, its present (1937) general manager; Joseph C. Lesser, treasurer of Alfred A. Knopf, Inc.; W. E. Kelly, assistant to the solicitor to the Postoffice; Paul L. Martin, editor of the Lansing (Mich.) *State Journal;* Walter A. Morrow, formerly managing editor of the Lansing *Capital News* and now editor-in-chief of the Scripps-Howard Southwestern Group; the late E. F. Edgett, of the Boston *Transcript;* Miss Katherine Donovan, formerly of the Boston *Advertiser;* A. L. S. Wood, of the Springfield (Mass.) *Union;* C. H. Wilhelm, of the Haddon Craftsman, Camden, N.J.; Hamilton Owens, editor of the Baltimore *Evening Sun;* Paul Y. Anderson, of the St. Louis *Post-Dispatch;* Marquis W. Childs, formerly of the United Press; Paul Palmer, formerly of the St. Louis *Post-Dispatch* and now editor of the *American Mercury;* C. W. Roberts, editor of the Farmington (Mo.) *Press;* Earle Bachman, formerly advertising manager of the *American Mercury;* the Rev. Raymond Calkins, president of the Watch and Ward Society at the time of the *American Mercury* case; Harrison Hale Schaff, of Boston; Mrs. Dorothea Brande Collins, circulation manager of the *American Mercury* in 1926; W. A. S. Douglas, formerly of the Baltimore *Sun;* Dr. Mary Parmenter, Harry F. Marks, H. Wadsworth Sullivan, W. M. Lamar, and Mr. Ehrmann.

The newspaper record that follows is unhappily very far from complete. The clipping bureaus missed many clippings (as the large number sent in by scores of volunteers proved), and various series of those that came in were segregated for one reason or another during the progress of the case, and then lost. Anyone who takes the trouble to look through the present collection will discover quickly that they show many glaring errors. Indeed, my own examination of them convinces me of the truth of something I have long suspected, to wit, that journalism can never be a really exact science. The reportorial brethren and sisters did their best, often under difficult conditions, but they were often careless about names, and sometimes they were far from careful about facts. In order to avoid a hopelessly lengthy record I have entered but one copy of each press association dispatch. Following it comes a series of the more interesting headlines it bore in other papers. Some duplications will be noted; despite the greatest care by my secretary, Mrs. Rosalind C. Lohrfinck, they crept in.

The pertinent legal documents are in the Appendixes, with references from the text. To them I have added a number of other records, including a characteristic selection from the hundreds of letters and telegrams that poured in. At the end of the clippings are some records of subsequent battles between the Comstocks and other of their victims, in Boston, in New York and elsewhere. The general success of our attack (though, as I shall show, we lost in the end) inspired many other persons to resist the fiats of organized wowserism, and for ten years following the *American Mercury* case there were frequent combats. Many of these flowed directly out of our own adventures. We had made the first really determined and pertinacious attack on the censorship of printing in Massachusetts, and other victims of it followed in our path. One of the results of our bout with Chase and company was an organized movement to change the archaic laws of the State. There were also, of course, many repercussions elsewhere. A curious by-product was the fact that, when Mary Ware Dennett was tried in Brooklyn, in April, 1929, for circulating her pamphlet, "The Sex Side of Life," all veniremen who admitted that they had ever read anything of mine were challenged by the prosecuting attorney, James E. Wilkinson. For ten years after 1926 no such trial went on anywhere in the United States without some mention in it of the *American Mercury*. To this day the case seems to be well remembered.

I have tried to make this record as objective as possible, and no pains have been spared to insure its fairness and accuracy. But it is written, of course, from the standpoint of one who is admittedly strongly opposed to all sorts of censorships, whether official or volunteer. I believe that any man accused of circulating indecent literature should have his day in open court, and that until he gets it he should be unmolested by any sort of intimidation. Every censorship, however good its intent, degenerates inevitably into the sort of tyranny that the Watch and Ward Society fanatics so long exercised in Boston. But it is always hard to break even the worst of such tyrannies down. The American people still show a Puritan strain, and plain-speaking is congenitally abhorrent to vast numbers of them. As I write (1937) there is a movement afoot to abolish the Postoffice censorship that we fought so bitterly and so vainly, but it will probably take a good many more years to dispose of it. The Customs censorship was modified by Congress in 1935 or thereabout, following a series of devastating decisions by enlightened Federal judges, but the Postoffice censorship still flourishes, albeit the present law officers of the Department are not as bold and shameless as the Solicitor Donnelly whose story is told in this chronicle.

I have left instructions that these volumes are to be deposited, after my death, in the New York Public Library. It specializes in the literary history of the United States, and I have hitherto given it a number of my letters from authors, and shall give it more hereafter. It is conceivable that this detailed narrative of the "Hatrack" case may some day interest an historian of American culture in the early Twentieth Century. I have had a lot of fun putting it together.

Baltimore, December, 1937.   H. L. Mencken.

I

THE assault upon the *American Mercury* for printing Herbert Asbury's "Hatrack" was certainly not unanticipated in the office of the magazine. Since its first issue, in January, 1924, it had been decidedly out of favor with the Puritans of the country, East, West, North and South, and had devoted a great deal of its space to exposing and ridiculing them. Among its contributors had been some of the most conspicuous foes of the blue-nose moral scheme, for example, Clarence Darrow, Senator James A. Reed of Missouri, James Branch Cabell, Albert Jay Nock, and Margaret Sanger, the prophetess of birth-control. There had been many demands in the religious press, and even in the newspapers, that it be suppressed, and at frequent intervals it had been barred from the news-stands of various communities, though there was never anything in it that could be described, with the remotest approach to accuracy, as subversive of civilized decency. In its department of "Americana," made up of printed imbecilities gathered from all parts of the country, there were many amusing examples of Puritan intolerance and hypocrisy.

Those were the palmy days of comstockery in the United States, and the professional comstocks recognized the magazine as an uncomfortable and perhaps even dangerous opponent. I myself was also on their blacklist, for I had taken an active hand against them in the defense of Dreiser's "The 'Genius'" in 1915, of Cabell's "Jurgen" in 1919, and of other books at other times. The *American Mercury* did not denounce the wowsers in a pontifical manner; its plan was to proceed against them satirically and they writhed under the attack. Next to John Sumner, the successor of the original Comstock in New York, the most potent and impudent of them at the time was the Rev. J. Frank Chase, secretary of the New England Watch and Ward Society of Boston. This organization had been formed in 1876, in the early days of Comstock's great crusade, and among its subsequent supporters were some of the principal Puritan clergy and laity of Boston, including various Cabots, Coolidges, Lowells, Quincys, Bowditches, Wigglesworths and Ameses. One of its vice-presidents, for 1925–26, was Dr. Charles W. Eliot, until 1909 president of Harvard. Chase, who became its secretary in 1907, at $3000 a year and expenses, after seven years of the meager life of a Methodist preacher, quickly perfected an extremely effective technic for getting his mandates obeyed. He seldom had to go to court, for it was well understood in Boston that judges and juries (the former often Puritans and the latter predominantly Irish Catholics) were almost invariably disposed to give him whatever he wanted. Instead, he proceeded by organized terrorism. Whenever a book fell under his displeasure he notified a body called the Boston Booksellers' Committee, and it immediately warned all the booksellers of the town that he "believed" there were "passages" in the book that would be "held by our courts to be in violation of the statutes." These passages were never nominated, and there was no discussion of the matter, and no chance for the publisher or author to be heard. The craven booksellers accepted Chase's fiat without the slightest question, and those who did not at once return their supplies of a banned book to the publisher hustled them under their counters and sold them thereafter only to known and trusted connoisseurs of pornography. The list of books thus banned was almost endless. It included much of the salient fiction of the time, for example, Cabell's "Jurgen," Sherwood Anderson's "Many Marriages," Aldous Huxley's "Antic Hay," and many of the books of Dreiser. The more civilized Bostonians were shamed by the spectacle that the town made before the country and the world, but the booksellers yielded their necks to Chase. The alternative was a summons to court and a probable conviction, with a heavy fine and maybe even a jail sentence following—a large risk for men whose interest in any given book could seldom be large.

Chase operated upon the magazine-sellers in a similar manner. He never went to court if he could help it. Instead, he notified a body called the Massachusetts Magazine Committee, representing the magazine wholesalers and chain-retailers of the State, that this or that issue of this or that magazine was on his index, and the Committee could then be trusted to pass on the news to the newsdealers, and so work its suppression. If an occasional newsdealer was bold or stupid enough to resist, he was fetched with a warrant and usually got a stiff fine. These dealers were almost always poor men, and the chance of losing $100 or more (or even going to jail) as the price of a few five- or ten-cent profits was enough to make most of them obey orders at once. A magazine publisher was almost helpless in the premises, just as a book publisher was helpless. The dealers simply refused to handle his magazine, and he could not force them to do so. Chase did not appear publicly in the transaction. There was seldom any legal evidence, available to the pub-

lisher, that he had had any hand in it. The New York comstocks looked upon the arrangement with undisguised envy.
The newsdealers and magazine wholesalers of their town
were much tougher fellows, and refused to be intimidated
so readily. Moreover, New York judges, district attorneys
and juries were generally hostile to the comstocks, as to
public nuisances, and often refused to lend them aid. Yet
more, the principal publishers of the country, on their home
grounds, were full of fight, and more than once the local
virtuosi of virtue had been sued for damages after a prosecution had failed.

Chase's astonishing power in Boston seemed to me to be
worth an article in the *American Mercury*, and early in 1925
I began to hunt for some one to write it. I approached several Boston newspaper men, but without success, for the
newspapers there, with few exceptions, were almost as completely intimidated by the Watch and Ward Society as the
booksellers and newsdealers. Indeed, Chase boasted in his
annual report for 1924–25, that "no book interdicted by the
Boston Booksellers Committee [*i.e.*, by Chase himself] has
been circulated by the book firms of this State, or advertised, or reviewed by our newspapers." Moreover, he also
boasted in private that he had forced the dismissal of John
Macy, erstwhile literary editor of the Boston *Herald*, for
denouncing his operations. I accordingly turned elsewhere,
and finally unearthed one A. L. S. Wood, a book-reviewer
for the Springfield *Union*, ambitious for larger deeds and
a wider audience. Wood went to Boston, had an interview
with Chase, gathered some material about him from others,
and wrote a brief article describing his practises. That article
was certainly not literature, and it was even no great shakes
as reporting, but it was the best I could get, and I printed
it, under the title of "Keeping the Puritans Pure," in the
American Mercury for September, 1925.

The magazine had barely come out when news arrived from J. J. Crowley, a magazine promotion agent of Boston, that Chase was furious and full of threats of revenge. In fact, he told the local wholesalers in undisguised gloating that the *American Mercury* would soon be banned from his diocese, and even talked grandly of having it barred from the mails, though on what ground he did not say. He was certainly not mollified when I printed a second article, under the title of "Boston Twilight," in the issue for December, 1925. This article was written by my assistant on the *American Mercury,* Charles Angoff, himself a Bostonian, and in the course of its description of the intellectual decay of the town Chase's activities were again mentioned. Nor was he pleased when he appeared a third time in the issue for April, 1926—in this case in an article entitled "The Methodists," dealing *inter alia* with his relations to the Board of Temperance, Prohibition and Public Morals at Washington. It was thus not surprising when, on March 28, word came from Crowley that Chase was prepared to ban the April issue, which had been on the stands since March 25. As usual, there would be no formal action. Chase had simply warned John J. Tracey, of the New England News Company, chairman of the aforesaid Massachusetts Magazine Committee, that the issue contained matter in violation of the law, and Tracey had passed on the word to all the other wholesalers, who had notified the newsdealers. "They are being quietly told," wrote Crowley to our circulation manager, Mrs. Dorothea Brande, "to take the April number off their counters." On March 30 the fact was reported in a brief United Press dispatch from Boston. Chase, following his invariable practise, did not communicate with us, and we were of course offered no opportunity to oppose his fiat. But he was departing from precedent by appearing in the matter openly, and even specifying the precise ground of his complaint. His objection, he said, was to an article called "Hat-

April 10, 1926

Chickasha (Okla.) Express

Magazine Boss Is Fighting to Have His Paper Mailed

(By The Associated Press)

Dubuque (Ia.) Herald

FEDERAL BAN HITS MERCURY

Postal Officials Bar It From Mails

Miami (Fla.) News

MAIL EMBARGO MOVES MENCKEN TO SEEK RULING

Editor Asks Court Hearing After New Bars Magazine

Deland (Fla.) News

POSTAL OFFICERS BAR MAGAZINE FROM THE MAILS

Story on Moral Conditions in Small Towns Responsible

Houston (Tex.) Post

MAGAZINE EDITOR SEEKS HEARING

Mencken Believes American Mercury Should Not Be Barred From Mails.

Sioux Falls (S.D.) Leader

AMERICAN MERCURY MAILED BUT NOW HAS BEEN BARRED

Dubuque (Ia.) Times

SMALL TOWN MORALS TALE IS OBSCENE

Magazine Publishing It Barred From Mails, But Too Late

Jacksonville (Fla.) Times Union

Mencken Will Ask Hearing On Mail Ban

Wants to Know Why Postal Officials Barred His Magazine.

Norfolk (Va.) Ledger Dispatch

Mencken's Magazine Is Barred From The Mails

New York April 6

On this page, as well as others to follow, a sampling of the multitude of clippings from Mencken's "Hatrack" scrap-books is shown. Some have yellowed to the point where photocopies are only partly legible. The sources and the dates of the clippings are in Mencken's handwriting.

rack," by Herbert Asbury, which he described, in a statement given to the Boston papers, as "immoral" and "unfit to be read." He went on:

> [It] viciously intimates that the preaching against immorality by the clergy acts as a boomerang, and that by warning their congregations against existing evils the ministers of God thereby indirectly suggest visits to these places of sin. Word pictures of alleged conditions are painted in filthy and degrading descriptions.

Copies of Chase's notice to Tracey seem to have been sent to the wholesalers in other Massachusetts towns, for reports that the magazine had been withdrawn by local news companies came the next day from Fall River, Worcester, Springfield and New Bedford. From Concord, N.H., there arrived news that the W.C.T.U., following Chase's example and perhaps at his instigation, was distributing a circular calling on the State newsdealers "to return copies of the magazine to the publisher."

The news companies and other wholesalers, having had bitter experience with him in the past, were generally quick to follow Chase's orders, but many of the retail newsdealers chose to risk the possible penalties of selling out the small stock in hand. Most of them succeeded in doing so before noon of March 30, for the announcement of the ban in the papers of that day made a brisk demand for the magazine. But others still had copies in the late afternoon, and Chase's agents went about threatening them. One of them, a Greek named Felix Caragianes, with a stand in Harvard Square, Cambridge, was actually arrested.

II

MY first inclination was to treat the matter lightly. After all, the April issue had been on the Boston news-stands nearly a week, and was virtually sold out, and all the mail subscribers in the Boston area had long since received the magazine. Moreover, I had expected some sort of reprisal by Chase, and was mildly amused by the fact that he had been foolish enough to base his action on an article so obviously innocuous as "Hatrack." When the United Press called me up on March 30 I contented myself with a brief statement describing the cause of his animus, denouncing him as a buffoon, and expressing the opinion that the majority of Bostonians really preferred *Hot Dog* to any intelligent magazine. Boston, in those days, was a notoriously poor magazine town. Its proletarians (mainly Irish or French Canadian Catholics) read the pulps, and its intelligentsia were still in the *Atlantic Monthly* stage of *Kultur*. The *American Mercury,* which had reached a circulation of 80,500 by April, 1926, was read relatively little in the Boston area.

But as I reflected upon the matter it became evident that

something would have to be done, for if Chase were permitted to get away with this minor assault he would be encouraged to plan worse ones, and, what is more, other wowsers elsewhere would imitate him. During the day I discussed the matter at length with my two associates, Alfred A. Knopf, who was the publisher of the *American Mercury*, and his father, Samuel Knopf, who was its business manager. We came to the conclusion that we should consult counsel. The names of several New York lawyers were considered, and in the end we decided to call in Arthur Garfield Hays, who had been one of the attorneys for the defense in the Scopes trial at Dayton, Tenn., in July, 1925. I had covered that trial for my old paper, the Baltimore *Evening Sun*, and had come into close contact with Hays, whose boldness and resourcefulness had impressed me favorably. Alfred and I went down to his office at 43 Exchange place late in the afternoon of March 30. He accepted the case and promised to get into communication with his Boston correspondents, Goulston and Storrs, and to have a plan of action ready by the next day. The next day Alfred Knopf and I saw him at his office again, and Leopold M. Goulston, head of the Boston firm, who happened to be in New York, was with him. He then proposed that he and I go to Boston, and that I there sell a copy of the April issue publicly, and defy Chase to order my arrest. The advantages of this scheme, he explained, were as follows:

    1. It would enable us to defend the magazine in open court, which would be difficult if not impossible in the case of Caragianes the newsdealer, who could be easily inveigled, in the face of a certain conviction and on the promise of a light fine, to plead guilty. (This was a trick, in fact, that Chase often worked.)

    2. My defiance would direct public attention to the attempt to suppress the magazine, and arouse those Bos-

tonians who were ashamed of the Chase censorship and eager to find a stick to flog it with.

3. The fact that I was a citizen of Maryland would enable me to appeal to the Federal court in Boston for relief in equity against Chase's assault on my good name and property. Caragianes could not so proceed against him, for disparate citizenship was necessary in order to invoke the Federal courts.

Hays often represented the American Civil Liberties Union in Court, and had had a great deal of experience in fighting censorships. He advised us that Chase, in all probability, was on friendly terms with the Boston district attorney, and would choose his judge in order to make sure of a conviction, but that we stood a good chance of winning on appeal, for it was difficult to imagine a court of any dignity holding "Hatrack" obscene. I asked him what the penalty might be if we lost in the end, and he said it could be as much as two years in prison. This possibility, I confess, was not pleasant to contemplate, but I decided to risk it. If my mother were still living I think I'd have hesitated, for she was given to affectionate worrying about her children, and my trial would have distressed her immensely. But her painful illness had been ended by death on December 13, 1925, and I was now free to take chances, and in fact somewhat eager for adventure.

It was accordingly arranged that Hays and I should meet in Boston on Monday morning, April 5—one week after the suppression of the magazine—, and that I should there sell a copy of the April issue on the Common, and defy Chase to order my arrest. This plan was announced to the press associations on April 3, and the morning newspapers reported it the next day. I had returned to Baltimore meanwhile, and remained there until Sunday evening, April 4, when I set out for Boston accompanied by W. A. S. Douglas, a correspondent of the Baltimore *Sun*. We traveled by the Federal Express, and had to turn out a little after seven in the morning. When we got to the Copley-Plaza Hotel we found a number of Boston reporters waiting for us. Hays was already in town, and had been in further consultation with Goulston and Storrs. He and I went to the office of the firm at 80 Federal street, and there met Herbert B. Ehrmann, one of the partners. Goulston was still in New York, and it was Ehrmann who served as our Boston adviser from that time forward.

Ehrmann told me that the first business in hand was to take out a pedlers' license. It had to be obtained from the Superintendent of Pedlers in the Boston Health Department, and getting it took some time. Meanwhile, Ehrmann had made contact with Chase, and tried to induce him to meet me in public and buy a copy of the April issue. It was a difficult job getting his consent. In the past he had always had his own way in Boston, but now an apparently belli-cose stranger had come to town to challenge him, with a lawyer of national prominence to brew the legal medicine, and he was considerably alarmed. A great light of publicity was already on him, and he suspected some trick to undo him. He proposed to Ehrmann that he be given until April 7 to decide whether he would fall in with the plans Hays had outlined, and pleaded that he had to consult the big-wigs of the Watch and Ward Society. But Ehrmann told him that we insisted on April 5, and that if he refused to meet me I'd launch a general sale of the magazine on the streets. So he finally agreed, though still very reluctantly, to meet me at 2 P.M. on April 5 at the corner of Park and Tremont streets—the celebrated Brimstone Corner. This arrangement was disclosed to the afternoon papers, and their noon editions came out with large headlines. I had given out a statement reiterating the charge that the whole attack on the *American Mercury* was due to Chase's resentment of "Keeping the Puritans Pure" and the other two articles belaboring him, and he had told the reporters once more that "Hatrack" was "bad, vile, raw stuff."

I got to Brimstone Corner a little before two o'clock, and found a huge crowd assembled—largely made up, it appeared, of Harvard undergraduates. With me were Douglas and John J. Mullen, the latter Knopf's chief book salesman. I had three copies of the April issue under my arm. Hays, coming by a different route by automobile, had fifty copies in a bundle, for general sale in case Chase failed to show up. I made my way to the agreed rendezvous with some difficulty, for the crowd was very dense, and called for Chase. A youngish man stepped up, said that he was Chase's assistant, and offered to buy the test magazine. When I refused to sell it to him he offered to produce evidence that he was the accredited agent of the Watch and Ward Society, but I still refused, and demanded that Chase appear in person. There was more delay here, but then cries of "Here he is!" were set up, and he slowly pushed his way toward me. With him were Captain George W. Patterson, chief of the Boston Vice Squad, and a young officer in plain clothes named Oliver W. Garrett. The actual sale took but a few seconds. Chase identified himself, I offered him a copy of the magazine, he handed me a silver half dollar, I bit it as if to make sure that it was good coin, and Chase said to Patterson, "I order this man's arrest." Garrett then tapped me on the arm, and the laborious march to police headquarters began. They were in a little court called Pemberton Square, only four blocks away, but Park street, which we had to traverse, was crowded from house-line to house-line, so we moved very slowly. Ehrmann, who had come up too late to be present at the sale, tagged along behind us. When we got to headquarters he was refused admission by Patterson, who insisted that one lawyer (Hays) was enough, and the two fell into a row which included some

When H. L. Mencken Was Pinched

Here's part of the crowd that magazine editor H. L. Mencken (in circle) attracted when he was arrested at Boston for purveying "indecent literature." In court a few hours later Mencken was acquitted.

The arrest.

show of fisticuffs. Patterson, in fact, was very bellicose, and seemed much upset by the yells of the crowd, which was plainly hostile to Chase. When we finally got into the little headquarters building I was led to the second floor by Garrett, and there booked by Lieut. Daniel Hines on a charge of violating Chapter 272, Section 28, of the Public General Laws of Massachusetts by possessing and selling obscene literature.

Save for Patterson, the police were very amiable, especially Garrett and Hines. Patterson, still fevered, espied Douglas with a copy of the magazine under his arm, and arrested him at once. Douglas protested bitterly that he was not offering it for sale, that he was present in the character of a newspaper reporter, and that if he were detained it would interfere with his work. But Patterson, obdurate, exclaimed "He's got the filth in his hands!," and insisted that Hines book him. Making no progress with Patterson, I appealed to Chase, who had come into the room, and he joined me in arguing that Douglas was an innocent bystander, and should be released at once. But it took some time to convince Patterson, who declared that he had no authority to release a prisoner booked on so serious a charge. Finally, he hit upon the masterly device of changing the charge to what he called S.P., *i.e.*, being a suspicious person. If Douglas would consent to this, he said, and would agree to sign a document absolving him (Patterson) of all legal liability for laying the original charge, he would call it quits. Douglas, eager to reach a telegraph office with a dispatch for the *Evening Sun,* consented at once, and after the cops had laboriously drawn up the document and he had signed it, he made off at a run.

As soon as this comedy had been disposed of I was taken to the Central Municipal Court nearby and formally arraigned. It was necessary, it appeared, for one of the judges of the court, of which there were half a dozen or more, to issue a warrant. When we got to the place there was a mysterious delay, and we were told that the judges were in consultation. Finally, one of them, William Sullivan, emerged, and I pleaded not guilty to both charges—possession and sale. Sullivan thereupon signed the warrant, and held me for trial. Patterson, apparently at Chase's suggestion, demanded that the trial be postponed for a week, but Hays objected vigorously, maintaining that the evidence was all present in the magazine, that no witnesses were necessary, and that a wait of a week would be a hardship to us. In the end Sullivan set our hearing for 10 A.M. of the next day, April 6. A policeman stepped up to say that the Superintendent of Police, Michael H. Crowley, would be content if I were released on my own recognizance. This was done, the surety being fixed at $500. I signed no bail bond.

After this I went to Ehrmann's office in Federal street, where a number of Boston reporters were waiting. Ehrmann and Hays had put in an hour in the morning drawing up a bill of complaint to be filed in the Federal court at Boston, praying for an injunction restraining Chase from interfering with us further. They now perfected this document, and took it to Judge George W. Anderson, of the United States Circuit Court of Appeals for the First Circuit, who was then sitting temporarily in the District Court. Judge Anderson was well known as a liberal, and Hays and Ehrmann wanted him to hear the case, but he refused to promise, giving as his reason that it might take some time and he was eager to return to his circuit. In order to get a standing in court we had to claim damages above $3000. We decided to ask for $50,000. Meanwhile, I wired to Stanley M. Reynolds, editor of the *Evening Sun* in Baltimore, requesting him to arrange for the Boston agent of the Fidelity & Deposit Company of Baltimore to furnish bail for me the next day, in case I should be convicted. This seemed highly probable, for the Boston Municipal Courts had always been very subservient to Chase. Reynolds replied at once, saying that the agent had been instructed by telephone to "furnish bail in any amount without security," and that he would see Hays and Ehrmann in the morning.

When I got back to the Copley-Plaza Hotel I found other telegrams. One was from Maury Maverick, of San Antonio, Texas, later a Congressman. It read: "I am with you. Run the jackasses to the cemetery." There was also one from R. F. Bradford, graduate secretary of the Harvard Union, inviting me to be the guest of the Union "at lunch or dinner on any date within the next ten days." I accepted for lunch on April 7, two days hence. R. S. Linscott, of the Houghton Mifflin Company, publishers, called up to invite me to dinner at the St. Botolph Club on April 6 as the guest of Ferris Greenslet, the head of the firm. He explained that Greenslet, whom I knew only slightly, wanted to show me that there were Bostonians who were ashamed of Chase, and eager to give me moral support. Henry Wadsworth Longfellow Dana, a professor at Harvard, came in with four or five of his students, offering assurances to the same purport. I also had calls from Harrison Hale Schaff, Isaac Goldberg and other old Boston friends, and arranged to lunch with Schaff the next day, April 6. He was a lawyer, but also dabbled in publishing, and his firm, John W. Luce & Company, had printed my first book in prose, "George Bernard Shaw: His Plays," back in 1905. Rather to my surprise I got no word from Ellery Sedgwick, editor of the *Atlantic Monthly* and my oldest friend in Boston. On April 23, long after I had left for home, I received a letter from him, saying, "I should have liked very much to see you during the anxious hours of your visit to Boston, but did not know how to get hold of you." A year or so later, when I was there again, he gave a dinner in my honor at the Tavern Club.

That evening we dined at Ehrmann's house. I was not

eager to go, for I wanted to discuss various phases of the case with Hays, and especially the proceedings in the Federal court. There was a somewhat large party, and it was after ten o'clock before Hays and I left. At the hotel we found Asbury and Mullen. Mullen, who was a Bostonian and still lived in Dorchester, was very pessimistic. He said that the district attorney of Suffolk county, Thomas C. O'Brien, was hot against us, and making threats to pack the jury if I asked a jury trial. He said that the "Boston Twilight" article, though it did not appear in the case, was having a powerfully adverse effect. Richard F. Fuller, manager of the Old Corner Bookstore and the dominant figure in the activities of the Boston Booksellers' Committee, was offering bets at fantastic odds that I'd be convicted, and in other ways fanning prejudice against me.

I was tired out, and after a nightcap with Douglas turned in. In view of Mullen's news sleep was somewhat delayed.

III

WHEN I got to the Central Municipal Court building the next morning, a little before ten o'clock,
I found my lawyers *non est*. They had gone to
see Judge Anderson again, to try to induce him to hear our
petition for an injunction against Chase, but found him still
unwilling to do so. It now appeared that he wanted some
other district judge to sit in the case in order to avoid dis-
qualifying himself if it were appealed to his circuit. Finally,
he set the hearing for April 12 at 10 A.M., a week hence,
and left the matter of the trial judge open. Hays and Ehrmann later told me that they had a very satisfactory palaver
with Judge Anderson, that he was a reader of the *American Mercury* and knew my books, and that he expressed the
opinion that "Mencken should be free to say any damned
thing he pleases."

But all this took time, and meanwhile I was in the Municipal Court without lawyers. The court officials were sym-
pathetic, and under cover of the delay and the resultant con-
fusion managed to do me a most valuable service. In fact,
they probably managed to get me acquitted. It had been

H. L. Mencken of "The American Mercury, braved Boston' police who had prohibited the sale of his magazine because of an article it contained. At left is Arthur Garfield Hays, his attorney; at right, the officer who arrested Mencken as a test case

arranged by the police, apparently at Chase's instigation, that I should appear before Judge Michael J. Creed, an Irish Catholic who was notoriously friendly to the Watch and Ward Society, and had fined or jailed many of its victims. But on the specious plea that Creed's docket was over-crowded, the officials quietly moved me to the court of Judge James P. Parmenter, and there I lingered for an unhappy half hour, waiting for my name to be called and my lawyers to appear. While I waited a young lawyer named John Gaston, quite unknown to me, accosted me in the courtroom and offered to serve as my counsel in case I should be called before Hays and Ehrmann arrived. In some desperation I accepted his offer, and we fell into conversation. He said that he had been an assistant district attorney under O'Brien, and that he had heard from a former colleague, still in office, that O'Brien was very hostile to me, and talking loudly about sending me to jail. He suggested that, inasmuch as O'Brien would go out of office in November, we try to postpone my trial over the Summer, on the theory that O'Brien's successor, whoever he might be, would be measurably less vicious. While this exhilarating conversation was proceeding Hays and Ehrmann finally hurried in, and at 10.45 my case was called.

It was not tried from the trial table. On the theory, so I learned, that the evidence was obscene and hence unfit for the ears of the spectators gathered in the courtroom, we were called up to the bench, and all testimony and argument went on *sotto voce.* The judge moved over to a corner, and there, in a little group, we stood. In the group were Hays, Ehrmann, myself, Chase, one of Chase's assistants, his attorney, John W. Rorke, and a few reporters. The rest of the people in the dark and shabby room craned their necks and stretched their ears behind us. The place was packed, though the catchpolls had made some effort to keep out all persons not directly concerned. There were many reporters present, some of them not assigned to the case, but appearing out of curiosity—in a few instances, far from friendly. There were also a number of photographers, and many photographs were taken. Also, there were two representatives of the Fidelity and Deposit Company of Baltimore, ready with bail in any amount.

Rorke, a tall, gaunt, seedy-looking fellow, had a handwritten, dog's-eared brief that had plainly seen hard service, and he referred to it very often. He began the proceedings by denouncing me in a violent manner as a corrupter of youth and a deliberate flouter of decency. He said that the law I was charged with violating had been passed "largely at the instigation" of "persons of my [his] persuasion," apparently meaning Catholics. He argued that inasmuch as Asbury had said in "Hatrack" that the effect of revivals on the youth of Farmington, Mo., was bad, the effect of reading about them would be to debauch the youth of the whole country. The formal evidence followed. Patterson, the indignant cop, was the first witness. He testified to my sale of the magazine at Brimstone Corner, and handed up the copy of it that Chase had bought, and the half dollar that he had paid for it. He swore that I had sold more than one copy—a lie. Chase followed. He said that he had first heard of "Hatrack" when an unnamed friend brought a copy of it to his house. On reading it, he sent to Harvard Square for a copy, and the arrest of Caragianes in Cambridge followed. He added that he had shrunk from the public scandal of the transaction at Brimstone Corner, but that I had insisted on it.

That concluded the case for the prosecution. Hays opened for the defense by putting me on the stand. I testified as to the usual contents of the magazine, and mentioned some of its contributors—a bishop, a United States Senator, and so on. I pointed out that it sold for 50 cents a copy, and was thus not generally circulated, and that its readers were mainly persons of some education, and included many well-known men and women. I explained that I had come to Boston to challenge Chase because his arrest of Caragianes left me no other method of defending my property and clearing my name. My testimony became an argument. I argued that Chase's customary method of proceeding was grossly unfair and disingenuous—that if anyone should be prosecuted for circulating an offending magazine it should be the responsible editor or publisher, and not some ignorant and helpless newsdealer. I contended that "Hatrack" was not in fact obscene within any rational meaning of the law, that the *American Mercury* never printed salacious matter, and that my own attacks upon comstockery had been directed solely at its raids upon serious and meritorious publications. The judge sat listening in silence—an old man with a scrubby gray mustache, wrapped in a much wrinkled black gown. Only once did he interrupt the hearing of the testimony. Then it was to agree with an objection by Rorke that the intent of "Hatrack" was immaterial—that however lofty an author's aim, his writings would have to be judged by their overt indecency or lack of it.

When I stepped down Hays recalled Chase for more particular testimony about the arrest of Caragianes, but it yielded nothing of importance. The next witness was a volunteer, H. Wadsworth Sullivan, a young Boston lawyer and the son-in-law of former Lieutenant-Governor Edward P. Barry of Massachusetts. He said that he was a recent graduate of the Yale Law School, and that students there had been put, in his time, to studying an article on divorce, printed in the *American Mercury* and written by William Seagle, a New York attorney. He said that they had been given credits for their familiarity with it. He added that Charles Evans Hughes, in a lecture at a law school, had once mentioned the magazine with approbation. Douglas followed, to testify about his unhappy encounter with Captain Patterson. His testimony, of course, was irrelevant, but it threw a certain light on the methods of Chase and his janissaries, and Hays managed to get it in before Rorke awoke. Rorke was no match for Hays. A stuffy and obviously stupid fellow, he managed his case badly, and got by far the worst of it in the argument at the end.

The last witness was Asbury. The plan of putting him on the stand had not occurred to Hays until we got to Boston on April 5, the day before the trial. He was then on the staff of the New York *Herald-Tribune,* and I called him up at the office of the paper. He turned out to be on vacation, but I was lucky enough to catch him at his home in Brooklyn, and he came up to Boston by sleeper, arriving early on the morning of April 6, a few hours before the trial began. Asbury's testimony was mainly to the effect that "Hatrack" was true in fact—that he had been brought up at Farmington, Mo., knew the original Hatrack, and had not exaggerated in his account of her operations. Hays made the most of Asbury's name—a name very famous in Methodist history. There was some discussion of Asbury's relation to Francis Asbury (1745–1816), the first Methodist bishop to be ordained in America, but the reporters seem to have listened inattentively, for some of them reported next day that he was a direct descendant of the bishop. When this story got about the country it greatly upset the Methodists, who were well aware that the bishop had died a bachelor.

The arguments followed. Hays made a general attack on comstockery, and maintained that the constitutional guarantee of free speech and a free press was menaced by it. "The fundamentals of American liberty," he said, "are involved in this case, and we appeal to this court as one of the bulwarks of the Bill of Rights." Rorke, often consulting his shabby brief, made the classical comstockian reply—that license was not liberty, and that the high price of the *Ameri-*

can Mercury, its limited circulation, and its appeal to an educated audience did not exempt it from the operations of
the law. Hays, in rebuttal, argued that the proof of the
pudding was in the eating, and that the court would have
to judge "Hatrack" by reading it. "Your honor," he said, "must
discover in your own mind whether reading it tends to
arouse lascivious thoughts." Hays was much smarter than
Rorke, and in the end forced him to concede that there was
nothing obscene about the language of "Hatrack"—that the
case of Chase was grounded wholly on the content of the
article, and not on the terms in which it was written. Rorke,
in closing, turned without previous notice to the department of "Clinical Notes" in the April issue, alleging that
a discussion of sex therein was immoral, but he did not press
the point.

Judge Parmenter sat through all this wearing an expression
of profound judicial calm. He interrupted the arguments
very seldom, and then only to state the law. I regarded him
somewhat uneasily. At this time I knew nothing whatever
about him, and had accepted the last-minute transfer of the
case from Judge Creed's court at its face value. I assumed
that Parmenter, like the rest of the Municipal Court judges
of Boston, was disposed to play the game of the Watch and
Ward Society. When he announced that he would read the
magazine and be ready with his decision at 9.30 the next
morning, April 7, I was half reconciled to a verdict of guilty
as an inevitable fact. The Boston reporters, a generally infe-
rior lot, appeared to know no more about Parmenter than
I did. The local correspondent of the New York *Herald-
Tribune* mistook him for Chief Judge Wilfred Bolster of the
Municipal Court, and so did the Associated Press representative.

After the hearing I had lunch with Schaff, Mullen and
Douglas. While we were at table a Jewish lawyer, known

to Schaff, came up. He predicted confidently that Parmenter would pass the buck by holding me for trial in the Criminal Court, and advised me to consult one John P. Feeney, a criminal lawyer whom he described as of great political influence. Schaff and Mullen were also sure that I'd be held for trial: they said that it was unheard of for a Municipal Court judge to flout the Watch and Ward Society by dismissing a prisoner out of hand. Neither of them knew anything about Parmenter. I put in the afternoon catching up with delayed mail, forwarded from Baltimore and New York. Mullen brought in his two young sons to meet me. In the evening I dined at the St. Botolph Club—one of the holy places of the Boston Brahmins—as the guest of Greenslet. Present: Greenslet, Linscott, Samuel Merwin the novelist, Edward Weeks, Jr., then associate editor of the *Atlantic Monthly,* Ira R. Kent of the Houghton Mifflin Company, and a man whose name I forget. Mullen came in later. Greenslet told me that Fuller, of the Old Corner Bookstore, was still offering bets that I'd be convicted. He said that opinion in Boston was virtually unanimously to that effect. Parmenter, he said, (and I heard it for the first time) was neither a Methodist, nor a Catholic, but a Unitarian. That seemed to be something, but someone added that not a few Unitarians were in the Watch and Ward Society. The dinner-party was not too cheerful. When it broke up Mullen and I went back to the Copley-Plaza Hotel. Mullen was still very pessimistic, but full of fight. He said that he'd be willing to risk his whole Massachusetts book business in order to help me. He was very bitter against Fuller, the best of all his customers. Fuller, he said, was in the habit of demanding special discounts from publishers on the plea that he had influence with Chase, and could protect books against suppression. He expatiated at length upon Fuller's character, with anecdotes from his experience. The fellow appeared, by his account, to be a shameless double-dealer and hypocrite. This judgment, as the following record will show, was well borne out by subsequent events.

While I was at the St. Botolph Club Hays was at Cambridge addressing the Harvard Liberal Club. Later in the evening he returned to New York by sleeper.

IV

I went to court the next morning with Ehrmann, Douglas and Schaff. There was only a small crowd present, made up chiefly of reporters. At 9.30 the clerk called me to the bar, and a moment later Judge Parmenter entered. Rorke was on hand, but, to my surprise, Chase was absent. The judge, on taking his seat, began pronouncing his decision at once. He had a copy of the magazine on his desk, but his remarks were extemporaneous. We all crowded up to hear.

As he proceeded I was quite bewildered. I had assumed almost as a matter of course that he would declare me guilty and hold me for trial, and when he began disposing of Chase's contentions one by one I began to wonder what would be left to justify that verdict. After four or five minutes the answer came, and with considerable dramatic effect. "I find," he concluded simply, "that no offense has been committed, and therefore dismiss the complaint." We all stood silent for a moment, with Rorke blinking and swallowing incredulously. The clerk finally broke the spell. Looking at me, he said: "You are free to go at once. Your bail is vacated. Next case."

But we did not leave at once. I recovered my wits enough to suggest to Ehrmann that he ask the judge for a copy of the decision, and he did so. It had been delivered, as I have said, extempore, and no stenographer was present, but it occurred to me that the judge might have put the substance of it in writing. He said that he had not, and refused somewhat testily to dictate it for recording. Ehrmann then asked him if he would read and approve a version prepared by those present, and after some hesitation he agreed to do so. This version was concocted later in the morning at Ehrmann's office, by Ehrmann himself, with aid from Douglas. I had no hand in the matter myself, for I was busy with newspaper reporters. They swarmed into Ehrmann's office, and I was left to deal with them. Some of them were visibly hostile. They represented papers friendly to Chase, and Judge Parmenter's verdict had robbed him of a great victory and their papers of a moral show. It seemed a good chance to spread some terror among the enemy, so I hinted at libel suits against papers that had maligned me, and at damage suits against Chase and his associates. I asked one of the reporters, in the hearing of all, to try to find out for me what real estate Chase owned, if any. Another reporter volunteered the news that he owned a good house in West Roxbury. I asked where it was and took elaborate notes. I also inquired about the financial responsibility of various directors of the Watch and Ward Society. Finally, I sent for a copy of the society's current annual report, and expressed great interest in the fact, disclosed therein, that it had an endowment fund of nearly $160,000. All this, I knew, would be carried to Chase by the blabbing reporters, and I was not without hope that it would upset him. Little did I suspect that he was already hard at work arranging a surprise reprisal of his own!

I had agreed to be the guest of the Harvard Union at lunch at 1 P.M., and at 12.30 a committee in an automobile called for me at Ehrmann's office. Its members told me that 200 students had subscribed to the lunch during the first hour after it was announced, and that an enormous crowd would be in attendance. It certainly was. When we got to the large hall in Cambridge called the Living Room of the Union every seat was taken, and scores of students unable to get places at the tables were in the gallery and massed along the walls. They did not know that I had been acquitted: the arrangements had been made on the assumption that I would be convicted, and the purpose of the gathering was to protest. When I told the news to Felix Frankfurter, who was to preside, he jumped up and announced it, and there was a great cheer. Then the lunch proceeded. At the end Frankfurter made a complimentary speech, and after him came Zechariah Chafee, Jr. I followed with a few remarks on the joys of fighting for freedom. After my brief speech I presented the Union with a large silk Maryland flag. It had been sent up from Baltimore on April 5 by Hamilton Ownes, editor of the *Evening Sun*, J. Edwin Murphy, its managing editor; and Harry C. Black, one of its principal stockholders—all vigorous proponents of the Maryland Free State idea. When I concluded, R. F. Bradford, graduate secretary of the Union, called for the Harvard cheer for me, and it was given three times *fortissimo*. Then I was photographed with him, and many of the boys came up to ask for autographs. In the yard outside newsreel and still cameramen later made some pictures, including a re-enactment of the presentation of the Maryland flag.

I returned to the Copley-Plaza in Boston at about 2 o'clock, and there found Goldberg and his wife, and Mullen. Mullen proposed that he and I proceed to New York at 5 P.M., and this we did. I had a pint or more of whiskey, and on the train Mullen and I drank it. We also ate a lavish dinner, ordered by him, consisting principally of a huge steak. When we got to the Algonquin Hotel, at about ten o'clock, Alfred and Blanche Knopf were there waiting for us, and in a little while Hays and his wife came in, bringing a Tennesseean interested in the Scopes case, whose name I forget. After a few drinks I went to bed, and had the first really comfortable sleep for a week.

The next day I spent at the *American Mercury* office, slaving away at my neglected editorial work, and trying to get through the enormous accumulation of letters, telegrams and newspaper clippings. In the evening I went to Hoboken, N.J., with H. E. Buchholz, an old Baltimore friend, and we had dinner at Meyer's Hotel, where the food was good and excellent bootleg beer was on tap. After dinner a newsboy came in with a late edition of the New York *Graphic*. In it I found a three-line item saying that the April issue of the *American Mercury* had been barred from the mails. The reason for Chase's disappearance from Boston thus became plain. He had slipped down to New York on the night of April 5, seen the postmaster there, John J. Kiely by name, and induced him to stir up the functionaries in Washington. It goes without saying that there had been no notice to the *American Mercury*, and hence no hearing.

V

THIS action was purely gratuitous and malicious. The whole April issue of the *American Mercury* had gone through the mails by March 20, and what is more, the issue had been examined and passed, not only by the postal authorities of New York, but also by those in Camden, N.J., where the magazine was printed. It was the rule of the Postoffice Department at that time (and still is: 1937) that copies of every publication enjoying second-class privileges should be submitted to the postoffice of entry prior to the mailing of every edition, in order to give the official smellers a chance to examine it for possible violations of the postal laws. Inasmuch as the *American Mercury* was printed in Camden and published in New York City, it had two second-class entries, and four copies of every issue had to be submitted to each postoffice—two for examination as to their advertising contents (the rate of postage varied with the proportion of advertising), and the others for examination as to the text. In the case of the April issue the four copies for the postoffice at Camden were sent in by the printers, the Haddon Craftsman, on March 17. Not

April 12, 1926

Pittsfield (Mass.) Eagle

Fined for Sale of Magazine, Appeals

CAMBRIDGE, April 12 (AP)—Felix Caragianes, a Cambridge news dealer, was found guilty in East Cambridge court today of selling obscene literature. The charge was based on sales of the April issue of the American Mercury which had been barred from sale made on complaint of the Watch and Ward society.

Caragianes was fined $100 by Judge Thurstone and appealed. He was defended by Arthur Garfield Hays of New York, who was counsel for H. L. Mencken, editor of the American Mercury, when the latter was arrested in Boston last week for selling copies of his magazine on Boston common.

The charges against Caragianes were laid before Mencken was acquitted in Boston municipal court on the charges of possessing and selling obscene literature.

Baltimore (Md.) Post

MENCKEN'S SUIT TO OPEN TODAY

BOSTON—Henry L. Mencken's suit for $50,000 damages against the New England Watch and Ward Society will open today before U. S. Judge George W. Anderson.

The suit is the second court action involving the Baltimore editor and Boston reformers as the result of an attempt to ban Mencken's magazine, the American Mercury. Mencken has asked a permanent injunction to prevent the Watch and Ward Society from interfering with the sale of his magazine.

Last week Mencken allowed himself to be arrested for selling a copy of the magazine to make a test case of his grievance. He sold the copy to the Rev. J. Frank Chase, secretary of the society. Later he was dismissed by Judge James Parmenter in municipal court, the jurist finding there was nothing to "corrupt the morals of the young" in a story called "Hatrack," which had caused a ban on the Mercury.

Mencken claims Chase asked the ban on the magazine because of "venom and malice," as a result of attacks made upon him by the Mercury.

Washington (D.C.) News

Mencken's $50,000 Suit Against Censors Opens

Magazine Editor Also Seeks Injunction Against Society

Bangor (Me.) Commercial

Cambridge Echo of Mencken Case

Modesto (Calif.) Herald

News Dealer Fined For Selling Mercury

Belvidere (Ill.) Republican

SOLD MERCURY; FINED

Des Moines (Ia.) Tribune

COPY AMERICAN MERCURY SELLS HERE FOR $8.50

A second copy of the April number of American Mercury owned by W. E. F. Schmidt, 1136 Twentieth street, this morning was auctioned off by Mr. Schmidt to an unnamed buyer for $8.50.

The auction was held on the sidewalk near Twentieth street and University avenue.

Mr. Schmidt sold his first copy Saturday for $5. The copy sold today was one that Mr. Schmidt had been renting for 50 cents a day.

H. L. Mencken, the editor, was recently arrested in Boston because of Herbert Asbury's article, "Hatrack," alleged to be salacious.

Boston (Mass.) Post

A DIME A LOOK AT "HATRACK"

Newsdealer Getting Profit From Copy of Mercury

OKLAHOMA CITY, April 11—A newsdealer here has the only copy of the American Mercury in town. He charges 10 cents a look to the hundreds who are eager to get a peek at the article called "Hatrack" that got the issue barred from the mails. It is reported that he made more money in one day with his single copy of the forbidden magazine than from the profits accrued from the rest of his periodicals.

a word of complaint came from the postoffice, and the mailing of the whole issue was completed on March 20. In the same way four copies were submitted to the postoffice in New York, and no suggestion was made by anyone there that the issue was unmailable. All the copies commonly mailed from New York had been cleared by March 25.

These postoffice examinations were by no means merely formal. It was common for magazine editors and publishers to be summoned to the main Postoffice in New York to explain something that had lifted the hair of a sensitive functionary. In February, 1921, Nathan and I had had such an adventure with the *Smart Set* for that month. The cover of the magazine showed a pair of perfectly harmless grotesque figures, both female, dancing. One of them wore a girdle from which several appendages dangled. It would be difficult to imagine a more innocent picture, but the lubricious imagination of the smellers in the New York Postoffice convinced them that one of the appendages resembled a quiescent virile member, and they accordingly held up the whole issue of the magazine. When Nathan got wind of this through the American News Company (no notice was served on us), he rushed to the Postoffice to protest—and narrowly escaped being handed over to the police. The chief smeller, secure in his authority, waived aside the argument that the effect of the picture, such as it was, was purely accidental, and that no one else had noticed it—not the artist, nor the editors, nor the engravers, nor the printer. He insisted that sending the cover through the mails would wreck the morals of the country, and it took Nathan three hours to persuade him to lift his ban. Even so, he did so very unwillingly, and with solemn warnings that if we offended again, the full force of the Federal government would come down upon us.

In the case of the ban on the *American Mercury* it took several days to find out just what had happened. Chase, it appeared finally, knew Judge Parmenter much better than we did, and judged correctly, from what went on at my trial, that I would be acquitted. So he decided, without waiting to hear the verdict, to go to New York at once, and try to enlist the aid of Kiely, who was a notorious ignoramus and very friendly to wowsers. Chase traveled by the Fall River Line, and reached New York early the next morning, April 6. Whether or not he was accompanied by his colleague, John S. Sumner, of the Society for the Prevention of Vice, I could never find out, but at all events he saw Kiely himself during the morning, and easily induced him to refer the April issue to Horace J. Donnelly, solicitor to the Postoffice at Washington. Donnelly apparently spent the next day, April 7, examining the magazine. I judge from subsequent events that he was somewhat irresolute at the start, but on the day following, April 8, he was aided in deciding by the receipt from Harry S. New, the Postmaster General and his superior, of a copy of a resolution passed that day by the Chamber of Commerce of Farmington, Mo., the scene of "Hatrack," calling upon him (New) to bar the April issue from the mails. New was a politician ever eager to oblige, and Donnelly was a bureaucrat who knew on which side his bread was buttered. That afternoon at 4.40 he dispatched a telegram to Kiely saying: "Article Hatrack in April *American Mercury* is unmailable under Section 470 Regulations." As I have said, we received no notice from him, nor from Kiely. Our first word of his action came from the newspapers, which reported that it had been announced in Washington by his assistant, Walter E. Kelly.

This assault from the rear, of course, would have to be met, but for the moment Hays and I were so busy that we could give it little attention. He was preparing to return to Boston on April 12, three days hence, to argue our application, filed in the Federal District Court there, for an injunction against Chase, and I was up to my ears in Baltimore in accumulated letters, telegrams and newspaper clippings. The last-named were pouring in in great number. They included not only reports of the overt proceedings in the case, but also a great many editorials, and most of the latter were hostile. The press of the country, indeed, was generally against us, and, as I shall show later on, some of the most influential papers were extraordinarily bitter. They denounced my challenge of Chase as a mere advertising dodge, and hinted that we were profiting hugely by a great increase in sales. As a matter of fact, we were profiting very little. The April issue, to be sure, was selling out, and orders were coming in for many thousands of extra copies, but we refused firmly to put the magazine back on the press, then or later. Copies were bringing high premiums, and many were being rented. But this familiar and inevitable effect of comstockery was not our fault, and all we could do was to refrain carefully from turning it to our advantage. This we did. In order to counteract the newspaper denunciations I decided to prepare a formal statement of our case, for circulation among editors. To this I applied myself as soon as I got back to Baltimore, and when it was ready Alfred Knopf had it mimeographed and sent out, marked "private" and "not for publication." I also wrote a special statement for the Baltimore *Sun* at the suggestion of Paul Patterson.

Hays, who was busy preparing for his argument before Judge Morton of the Federal District Court at Boston on April 12, sent his partner, David A. Buckley, Jr., down to Washington on April 9 to see Donnelly and find out what could be done with him. Buckley called me up at Baltimore at noon and told me that Donnelly refused to budge. I suggested that I'd like to tackle him myself, if only to find out what was in his head, and Buckley called back in a little while to say that Donnelly would see the two of us on Monday, April 12. But when Hays heard of this arrangement he objected, for he wanted to be present at the palaver, and he had to be in Boston on April 12. So Buckley arranged with Donnelly that we should all meet at the latter's office in Washington on Thursday, April 15, at 9.30 A.M.

Meanwhile, we were considerably entertained by a fresh woe. In the *American Mercury* for May, then on the press, there was an article called "Sex and the Co-Ed," written by Bernard A. DeVoto, under the *nom de plume* of John August. It was a harmless enough article, arguing that the co-eds of the country were a great deal more virtuous than current report credited them with being, but it dealt with a subject that always inflamed wowsers, and so I asked Hays to read it. He expressed a fear that Donnelly might use it as an excuse to bar the May issue from the mails, and then take away our second-class privilege on the ground that we had missed two successive numbers, and were thus not "of continuous publication." This trick had been worked against various radical magazines during the Red hunt following the World War, and with disastrous effects upon them. The Postmaster General in those days was the notorious Albert S. Burleson, and the solicitor to the Postoffice was William H. Lamar, but Donnelly had served as a legal assistant under both of them, and would be familiar with the *modus operandi*. If our second-class privilege were taken away from us we'd be wrecked, for we'd then have to pay the full rate of ordinary postage on every copy of the magazine, however innocent its contents. To be sure, we'd have a hearing before Donnelly before the order was issued, but it was manifest that if he ever actually took steps to issue it that hearing would be only a mockery. Moreover, the experience of other magazines showed that appeals to the courts for relief from such oppressions seldom brought it. Unless one could prove that the Postoffice was animated by malice, which, legally speaking, was commonly impossible, they refused to intervene.

I therefore decided, in view of Hays's qualms, to scrap

the May issue—a costly and difficult business, for, as I have said, it was already on the press. Many thousands of copies, in fact, had been printed and assembled, with only the binding remaining to be done. But I called up my assistant, Angoff, in New York, and instructed him to make up a new issue, substituting a wholly innocuous article called "On Learning To Play the 'Cello," by Doris Stevens, for "Sex and the Co-ed." Angoff, on April 12, went to Camden, N.J., where the *American Mercury* was printed by the Haddon Craftsman, and there saw the new May number through. The last proofs of the electrotype plates were ready by midnight on April 13, and at 2 A.M. of April 14 the presses began to roll. The revised number, in an edition of 83,000, was quickly printed and bound, and a supply reached the American News Company on April 17, but two days late. This reprinting of a whole issue cost us at least $8,000—in fact, it cost us almost as much as all the other proceedings in the "Hatrack" case taken together. But it had to be done, for no trust whatever could be put in Donnelly's fairness and good faith.

The Haddon management had promised to destroy every copy of the suppressed number (save, of course, a few that we kept for possible future action), and I believe that it tried honestly to do so, but a number were bootlegged out of the plant by printers, and in a couple of weeks they began to be offered in New York at high prices. How the news was concealed from the newspapers I don't know, but concealed it was until May 1, when it was printed by the Camden *Courier,* owned by J. David Stern. The International News Service, a Hearst press association, sent out the story from Camden the next day, and for a week or more it occupied the newspapers throughout the country and gave our journalistic enemies a good chance to belabor us. Some of them reported that the expunging of "Sex and

the Co-Ed" had been ordered, not by me, but by Alfred
Knopf, and against my protest. This, of course, was not true.

On April 15, when I had my hearing before Donnelly
in Washington, I handed him, just from the press, a copy
of the revised May issue, and asked him for an immediate
verdict on it. He refused to have anything to do with it
unless it were submitted to him in the regular course by
some postmaster. On returning to Baltimore that evening
I wrote to him, saying that a copy would be filed at once
with the postmaster at Camden, accompanied by a request
that it be forwarded to Washington, and asking him to act
upon it promptly. The next day he replied, saying, "Upon
receipt of the copy I shall be pleased to give the case prompt
attention, and expedite the matter just as much as possible."
Four copies were filed by the Haddon Craftsman on April
16. When I had heard nothing from Donnelly by April 21,
I wrote to him again. He replied as follows under date of
April 24:

> The postmaster at Camden submitted a copy after a mail-
> ing had gone forward, and he was advised that he should
> not refuse to accept further mailing of that issue. He was
> told it must be understood by the publishers that responsi-
> bility rested upon them for any violation of law that might
> be involved because of any advertisement or other matter
> appearing therein.

The Haddon Craftsman received no notice from the postmaster at Camden that the May issue had been passed; they
were left to infer it. But on April 20 they received from
him a notice reading:

> Relative to all matter printed and sent out by you, it must
> be distinctly understood by the publishers that in deposit-
> ing copies of issues in the mails the responsibility rests upon

them for any violation of the law that might be involved because of any advertisement or textual matter appearing therein.

In other words, the postoffice demanded an advance copy of every magazine for examination, but did not announce its verdict to either the publisher or the printer (who usually did the actual mailing), and took no responsibility. A magazine that had been passed might be barred just as well as one that had not been passed. This notice to Haddon, I have no doubt, was prepared for the postmaster at Camden by Donnelly.

VI

AYS went to Boston on April 11 to argue our injunction case before Judge Anderson the next day in the Federal District Court. I remained in Baltimore, for I was overwhelmed by a flood of correspondence, and by the accumulated routine work of the magazine. Judge Anderson, when the hearing opened, decided to transfer the case to Judge James M. Morton, Jr., of the Federal District bench, explaining frankly, as reported by the Boston *Evening Transcript,* that, "as he sits in the [Circuit] Court of Appeals, he did not wish, by issuing an order in the District Court, to disqualify himself from hearing the case if it is appealed." Judge Morton was ready for the hearing after the noon recess, and it was finished late that afternoon. Hays and Ehrmann appeared for us, and Chase and the Watch and Ward Society were represented, not by the preposterous Rorke, but by a much better lawyer, Edmund A. Whitman, who also represented the Hotel and Railroad News Company. The Armstrong Company was represented, until it and the Hotel and Railroad News Company were dropped from the case with Hays's consent, by W. F. Garcelon, who took only a perfunctory part in the argument.

The proceedings began with a hearing on the motion of Chase and the Watch and Ward Society to dismiss the bill of complaint. Whitman opened. Judge Morton asked him at once what "special parts" of "Hatrack" were objected to, and he had to nominate them—something that Rorke had avoided carefully in my trial before Judge Parmenter. He said that he had discussed the article that morning with Judge Stone in Cambridge (of which more anon), and that Stone had been "impressed most" with the passage on page 481, beginning "Small town men" and running through to the end of the section, and with "the discussion of harlotry in small country towns" on pages 482 and 483. He also pointed to two passages in "Clinical Notes"—one beginning "Sex is" on page 493 and running to the end of the paragraph, and the other beginning with "Although the fact" on the same page and running to the end of the article on page 494. Judge Morton read these passages as they were named, but made no comment. Whitman and Hays then proceeded to argue at length, pro and con, with the judge frequently interrupting. After a while he said he would take under advisement the motion to dismiss the bill, and suggested that argument proceed on the application for an injunction. In the course of the latter Hays put Chase on the stand, and wrung from him a pretty clear account of the way in which the Watch and Ward Society operated. The debate then went on, and just before the close Whitman advanced an argument that was to be heard from the attorneys for the Postoffice later on—that no actual harm had been done to the *American Mercury* by the proceedings against it, but that, on the contrary, they had given it useful advertising.

"I think I read in a newspaper interview with Mr. Mencken," said Whitman, "that he does not care anything about the closing of the mails: the magazine is all distributed.

That is one reason [for refusing an injunction]. In the second place, I don't suppose this Court sits to issue injunctions where they won't do any harm [*i.e.*, where they are not actually necessary]. This is a case, with all due respect to my adversary, where he wants advertising. If he can go out and say the Court has issued an injunction, he can go out and say that this Court has read the article, and thinks it perfectly all right."

At this Hays was on his feet at once.

"I resent that," he declared. "That is not our purpose at all. There has been a demand for a million copies of this article in issue, and there is going to be no reprinting of the April number. That we have distributed. We are trying to prevent what we regard as an objectionable interference with our rights. Our May number is coming out. . . ." And so on.

Whitman thereupon fell into a capital blunder.

"If," he said, "they will submit to us the May number in plenty of time, we will notify them whether it is objectionable or not."

This astonishing proposal, of course, was all Hays needed to prove his whole case, and he leaped to the charge in high fettle.

"That," he exclaimed, "is an outrageous presumption. That is what I object to—that we should have to submit our magazine to these people, to find out whether we can distribute it in Massachusetts. It shows the whole situation. They want to be censors of our business, and they have no right to do it. We will put in what we want, and we ask you to have us arrested if there is anything in it that is improper, and nothing more."

"Not even give you a warning?" replied Whitman, weakly.

"No," roared Hays. "We don't want the warning."

This hearing was on April 12. Two days later Judge Morton announced his decision. It granted us our injunction, and sustained our complaint in every particular. After describing, as it has been described in this history, the *modus operandi* of Chase and the Watch and Ward Society, the opinion went on:

The injury to the persons affected does not flow from any judgment of a court or public body; it is caused by the defendants' notice, which rests on the defendants' judgment.

The result on the other person is the same whether that judgment is right or wrong, *i.e.*, the sale of his magazine or book is seriously interfered with. Few dealers in any trade will buy goods after notice that they will be prosecuted if they resell them. Reputable dealers do not care to take such a risk even when they believe that prosecution would prove unfounded.

The defendants know this and trade upon it. They secure their influence, not by voluntary acquiescence in their opinions by the trade in question, but by the coercion and intimidation of that trade through fear of prosecution if the defendants' views are disregarded.

In my judgment this is clearly illegal. The defendants have the right of every citizen to come to the courts with complaints of crime. But they have no right to impose their opinions on the book and magazine trade by threats of prosecution if their views are not accepted.

The facts that the defendants are actuated by no commercial motive and by no desire to injure the plaintiff do not enlarge their rights in this respect, though it may protect them under Massachusetts General Laws.

Of course, distributors have the right to take advice as to whether publications which they sell violate the law, and to act on such advice if they believe it to be sound. The defendants have the right to express their views as to the propriety or legality of a publication.

But the defendants have not the right to enforce their views by organized threats—either open or covert—to the distributing trade to prosecute persons who disagree with them.

On the same day the following injunction was issued:

DISTRICT COURT OF THE UNITED STATES
DISTRICT OF MASSACHUSETTS
Equity #2541.
THE AMERICAN MERCURY, Inc.
vs.
J. FRANK CHASE, *et als*

Interlocutory Decree for Temporary Injunction

This cause came on to be heard at this sitting of the Court on the plaintiff's motion for a temporary injunction, and was argued by counsel, and thereupon, upon consideration thereof.

IT IS ORDERED, ADJUDGED AND DECREED:

That until further order of the Court the defendants, J. Frank Chase and The New England Watch and Ward Society, their servants, agents and attorneys, are hereby enjoined from interfering with the sale and distribution of any future issues of the *American Mercury* by organized threat and intimidation, whether direct or covert.

By order of the Court.

Judge Morton also refused to dismiss our claim for $50,000 damages, and it remained on the docket, to be tried later, if we decided to call it up. Altogether, his decision was a severe blow to the Watch and Ward brethren, who had never been so badly beaten before. They were very much alarmed, especially Chase.

But the day was nevertheless not one of unmixed disaster for them, for in the morning they had succeeded in inducing Judge Arthur P. Stone, in the Third District Court of Eastern Middlesex at Cambridge, to find Felix Caragianes, the Harvard Square newsdealer, guilty. These proceedings showed why Chase had chosen Cambridge instead of Boston for his initial assault on the *American Mercury*, and why he resisted so stoutly when I proposed to drag him into the Boston area. Stone was very complaisant, and had obviously done business with Chase before. He admitted from the bench that "Hatrack" as a whole was "not so bad as painted," but said he thought it was bad enough to warrant the imposition of the $100 fine—the minimum under the law. Hays appeared for us at the hearing, and Whitman represented the Watch and Ward Society. Chase was present, but did not testify. The sale of a copy of the April issue was proved by W. C. Vien, an agent of the society, and Caragianes testified that he had sold 35 copies altogether. Whitman, in his argument, contended that "if Judge Parmenter had been a married man he would have never dared to go home after rendering his decision on 'Hatrack'." He insisted that "the article did have a tendency to corrupt youth," and argued that the fact that "the magazine was circulated among students" was "all the more reason why it should be suppressed." He then referred to "an article by Mencken on Prohibition," without further identifying it, and allowed virtuously that "he would never read the magazine again, for the article deliberately asked the people to violate the law." When the judge's decision was announced Hays at once entered an appeal, and Caragianes was released in his own recognizance.

The next day Chase returned to Cambridge and delivered a long speech on "The New Puritanism" at a luncheon of the Harvard Liberal Club. It was a somewhat pretentious statement of his philosophy, and included quotations from Dante (one in the original Latin), Tennyson and Kipling. Its language, in light of his ordinary bald prose, strongly suggested the hand of a ghost writer. He complained, rather surprisingly, that the Postoffice was not giving him as much aid and comfort as it might, and ascribed the fact to recent decisions by "certain Tammany judges" in New York. "A whole high-school class of unwedded mothers," he declared, "may be the result of a lascivious book." The Harvard Liberals, I was told later, heard him politely, but without visible enthusiasm. He did not mention the *American Mercury.*

VII

THE proceedings before Donnelly at Washington on April 15 were, of course, farcical, for Donnelly was both judge and defendant in the case. I went to Washington from Baltimore early in the morning, and met Hays and the Knopfs, Alfred and Blanche, in the lobby of the Shoreham Hotel. We were at Donnelly's office at 9.30, the hour he had set.

He received us politely, but without any show of cordiality. He turned out to be the living image of Calvin Coolidge, then in the White House, and it soon appeared that he was well aware of the fact and even apparently proud of it, for he gave an elaborate imitation of Coolidge's mannerisms, speaking sententiously and in a squeaky voice. There was some delay at the start, but by 9.45 the hearing was under way. No one was present in the large, bare, hideous room save Donnelly and his assistant, William C. O'Brien, Hays, the two Knopfs and myself. Donnelly sat behind a wide desk in judicial calm, speaking only seldom and then from the corner of his mouth. He had announced on April 9, after hearing Buckley, that the matter was "a closed issue," so the hearing was hardly more than moot, but nevertheless Hays waded in with great energy, citing endless court decisions and rehearsing all the arguments that he had already presented to Judge Parmenter, Anderson, Stone and Morton. He was becoming very glib by now, but nevertheless he made an error in one of his references to the authorities, and had to write to Donnelly the next day, correcting it.

At about ten o'clock another of the assistant solicitors, W. E. Kelly, came in and whispered to Donnelly, and Donnelly immediately suspended the proceedings and left the room. He was gone a long while, and meanwhile Hays and I palavered with O'Brien and Kelly. Both were young men—O'Brien a somewhat sombre fellow in horn-rimmed spectacles, and Kelly of a brisker type, with pompadour hair and a very earnest manner. It was plain after a little talk that both were sneakingly ashamed of the way we had been struck from behind. They admitted without much argument that the case against "Hatrack" was a feeble one, but sought somewhat lamely to justify the departmental regulation which denied a publisher a hearing before being barred from the mails. The excuse they offered was that it was sometimes necessary to act quickly, lest the country be flooded with pornographic horrors or Red propaganda. Hays replied that this was certainly not a fact in our case, for our April issue had already gone through the mails nearly a week before Donnelly's order was issued. The two assistants were trying to think of an answer to this when Donnelly saved them by returning.

It turned out that he had been called outside by a number of newspaper reporters, and that they wanted to get in. He asked us if we objected, and we answered certainly not. He seemed irresolute, saying that it was not the custom to admit the press to hearings, but in the end he relented and went out again to fetch the reporters in. They were ten or twelve in number, and included several that I knew very well—for example, Paul Y. Anderson, of the St. Louis *Post-Dispatch*, with whom I had covered the Scopes trial. Anderson told me later that the reporters had had an acrid row with Donnelly, who was apparently very much opposed to admitting them. Once they had prevailed against him, they remained until the end of the hearing, which ran to nearly 2 P.M.

It was plain enough that Donnelly's mind was tightly made up, and that no conceivable argument could move him. Indeed, it would have been dangerous for him to confess that he was wrong, for then we would have had good grounds for a suit against him personally. But Hays went on with the argument, laying great stress upon the decisions of Judge Parmenter and Morton that "Hatrack" was not actually obscene. Donnelly answered in his dry, clipped way that the Massachusetts statute and the Postal Act were different. Hays replied that the statute was wider than the act. Donnelly, of course, denied this and quoted a number of decisions that he believed sustained him. Hays was careful to take note of these decisions, for they would appear on appeal, and he wanted to be familiar with them. Finally, he argued that the *Mercury* was obviously not a common sex magazine, and could not be so considered and treated, for it did not reach idiots but was read largely if not mainly by well-educated persons, including many university professors. Kelly thereupon spoke up, arguing that I had often depicted professors as stupid, and that I had thus confessed that they were susceptible to lascivious suggestion. To this imbecile argument Hays made no reply.

Instead he turned to me, and suggested that I say something myself. I began by denouncing strongly, on grounds of common justice and common decency, Donnelly's action in tackling us from the rear without notice of hearing. He answered primly that he had nothing to do with it—that

April 12. 1926

Montgomery (Ala.) Advertiser

the actual culprit was the magazine, and it spoke for itself. I then mentioned common courtesy, but he waved it away. He proceeded to an argument that he apparently used often, for he stated it with surprising glibness, considering his general parsimony of speech. In substance, it was that, in case a bomb were found in the mails, the Postoffice had a clear right to throw it away at once, without notifying the sender or giving him any chance to explain its presence. I replied that this parallel was clearly faulty, for anyone could be damaged fatally by a dangerous bomb, and no one would be in favor of transporting it, whereas in the case of "Hatrack" there was a sharp difference of opinion, with many eminent authorities, including Judges Parmenter and Morton and salient members of the Harvard law faculty, standing irreconcilably against Donnelly himself. In view of this difference, I argued, he should not have acted without careful deliberation, and a fair hearing of our case. To this he made no answer.

I then charged formally that the whole proceedings, in so far as the Postoffice was concerned, had been set in motion by Chase, who was sweating for revenge, and had adopted the characteristic device of hitting me with an *ex parte* administrative order, obtained behind my back, after he had failed to reach me by open judicial process. Donnelly protested that he had had no communication with Chase—that the magazine had been submitted to him in the regular course by Kiely, the postmaster at New York. I replied that that was precisely our case—that Kiely had not moved until Chase had got after him—that the magazine was already through the mails when he acted, and had been passed by his regular smellers nearly two weeks before. I went on to argue that even the worst cancer quack got a hearing, though he was killing people by the score, whereas we had got none, though any damage we could conceivably do was already done. Moreover, the danger presented by the quacks was

obvious, urgent and universally recognized, whereas in our
case many highly respectable and responsible men were convinced that we were doing no damage at all. I then argued
that it was quite impossible to regard the *American Mercury* as a magazine devoted to pornography—that its general character was very far from that, and had been admitted
categorically by Judge Parmenter, and was not questioned
by any rational person. The worst we could be accused of,
I maintained, was a chance and unwitting invasion of the
law, and even if we were clearly guilty we at least deserved
the politeness accorded to the cancer quack.

I then brought up the odoriferous Rhinelander annulment
case, which had occupied the newspapers for months during
1925, and asked why Donnelly had not barred them from
the mails. Donnelly made no reply, and the following dia-
logue ensued:

> Mencken—Suppose I print a page from the newspaper
> accounts of the Rhinelander trial in my magazine, what
> then?
> Donnelly—We only cross bridges when we come to them.
> Mencken—That's just the answer I expected.

Donnelly changed the subject by producing a copy of the
San Diego (Calif.) *Herald,* a disreputable weekly that had
reprinted "Hatrack" without permission and in violation
of our copyright. He held it up and demanded to know
if I made any distinction between it and the *American Mercury*—whether I was prepared to admit, in case he let the
Mercury go, that he would also have to let the *Herald* go.
I answered that the difference between the two was obvious
to anyone. The *Mercury* was a reputable, serious, solvent
and respected magazine, selling at a high price and appealing only to reasonable people, whereas the *Herald* was a
low, cheap gutter sheet, printed solely for the prurient. I

argued that Donnelly was punishing us because a rogue had stolen our property, and had been caught using it for base ends. I pointed out that the Postoffice itself made a distinction between publications on the score of the audiences they were designed to reach, and cited the case of Dr. Kemp Malone, associate professor of English in the Johns Hopkins University, who had imported a copy of Ovid, and then resisted stoutly and successfully, with my assistance, when the postmaster at Baltimore, B. F. Woelper, Jr., undertook to confiscate it. Donnelly said somewhat wryly that Woelper had sent him my letters about the Malone case. I said: "But Malone now has his book." Donnelly: "Has he?" Plainly enough, my intervention in the Malone case had stuck in his craw, and helped to condition his attitude now.

He then read a long letter from some unknown person in the West, protesting against an article by James M. Cain, called "The Pastor," that I had printed in the *American Mercury* for May, 1925, a year before. The same letter complained of a piece of "Americana" in the same issue—a grotesque village ordinance in effect in Norphlet, Ark., forbidding adultery. I demanded the name and address of the writer, but he refused to give them to me. The letter argued that the *American Mercury* should be barred from the mails permanently, first on the ground stated and then on the general ground that it was hostile to revealed religion. I protested that it was unjust to put us on trial without giving us a right to confront our accusers, and that there was no law, and could be no law, forbidding us to publish other laws. To this Donnelly made no answer, save to speak vaguely of an unspecified court decision.

I closed with an effort to induce him to pass on the revised May number of the *American Mercury,* a copy of which I had put on his desk. He refused flatly, saying that he could consider it only on receipt of an inquiry from some postmaster, and in the regular course of business. I then told him that I wanted to file a formal complaint against it myself, alleging that it violated Section 211 of the Act of March 4, 1909, but he refused to accept the complaint. Finally, he suggested that it be filed with the postmaster at Camden along with the usual test copies of the number, and promised to give it consideration if the postmaster passed it on to him.

The hearing then terminated. On Donnelly's desk I noticed a copy of the *Atlantic Monthly* for March, 1926, with a marker in it, and also a copy of Ernest Hemingway's "In Our Times." Donnelly made no reference to them, and neither did I. There was, of course, no doubt about his decision. He had made his attitude plain throughout the hearing, and as we left he said to Hays: "I'll tell you frankly, Mr. Hays, that you haven't convinced me that this thing doesn't come within the statute." The reporters heard this, and at once sent out the news. The Knopfs, when the séance was over, went to a hearing on a proposed new Copyright Act, then in progress at the Capitol, and Hays and I went to lunch in the Senate restaurant with Senator Burton K. Wheeler of Montana. He was an old acquaintance of Hays's, but I had never met him before. There was some talk about Donnelly. Wheeler agreed with Hays and me that he was a ridiculous and somewhat pathetic figure—the perfect model of a third-rate bureaucrat, vain, cocksure and unintelligent. After lunch I went to Union Station, and there found the Knopfs. We traveled as far as Baltimore together, discussing our situation. I was, of course, eager to appeal to the Federal courts against Donnelly's decision sustaining himself, and Alfred Knopf agreed that it should be done. I got off at Baltimore and the Knopfs continued to New York. Hays returned there the same night.

The next day he sent Donnelly a letter correcting a legal

reference that he had made in error at the hearing, and presenting a last argument for a reconsideration of our case. The essential parts of it follow:

I do hope you men will give consideration to the arguments presented. I was at first upset at the thought of the difficulty of the human mind to reverse a point of view, but it occurred to me that we often have rearguments in court before a judge who not only has passed upon a matter but who passed upon it after having heard argument. Yet reversals are not uncommon.

Are not you men impressed by the fact that every man on the faculty of the Harvard Law School is of the opinion that this article does not violate the law and that that is the opinion of a very large percentage of lawyers? If there is a large difference of opinion (even though your opinion may be one way) is it quite fair to exercise the powers of government as though the case were a clear one? Is it not possible for government officials to err, if they err at all, on the side of freedom? In my work of the last few years, I have been impressed by the general attitude of the government toward restriction. The influence and the prejudice seem always that way.

In this case you have met the publisher. You know the kind of magazine he is producing. You have looked into the case again. You have the advantage of Judge Parmenter's decision and I hope have given considerable further thought to the matter. You men are the government. You know that if I get into court I shall have to face a very different question than that before you. I am aware that this is not a criminal proceeding, but the effect of punishment is still severe. The statute is a penal one and should be strictly construed. I think you agree that the method of procedure ought really to cause even greater caution than when a defendant has the usual opportunities to present his case before prejudgment. I do hope that where there is such a difference of opinion, the error, if it exists at all, will not be along the lines of restriction.

Receiving no answer to this, Hays wrote to Donnelly again on April 23. The next day Donnelly replied, saying that, "after further very careful consideration of the case, the department adheres to its original ruling that the April issue of the *American Mercury* is unmailable." On April 28 Hays filed suit against Donnelly and New in the Federal District Court at New York, asking for an injunction restraining them from carrying out that ruling.

VIII

BACK in Baltimore, I put in a couple of days reading the accumulated newspaper clippings and other records of the combat. It had been going on now for two weeks, and we had already appeared in three different courts, beside fighting our first battle with the Postoffice. The newspaper comments were predominantly against us—indeed, they were overwhelmingly so. The Boston *Herald* had led off on April 2, three days before I got to Boston, with a brief editorial that was obviously designed to give aid and comfort to Chase. "If the author [of 'Hatrack']," it concluded, "had any other purpose in writing than to appeal to a prurient impulse, always more or less latent in the community, such a purpose seems to us adequately disguised." In other words, we were clearly guilty as charged. The next day the *Herald* returned to the assault, this time with a counterblast to an editorial in our defense, printed in the New York *Evening World* the day before. The *Evening World* had correctly stated the thesis of "Hatrack" in these words: "that the ministers' preaching against immorality does more harm than good, by indirectly suggesting sinfulness to the congregation." The *Herald* denied this vehemently, and concluded with the following unctuous sentence: "New York rather prides itself on the possession of stronger stomachs than here are common, and to that possession the metropolis is quite welcome." On April 5, the morning before my arrest, the *Herald* delivered a third salvo. In this it compared me to Earl Carroll, a New York theatrical manager, lately arrested for displaying photographs of nearly naked chorus girls in his theatre lobby, and argued that there was nothing in my challenge of Chase save a publicity stunt.

The *Herald,* in those days, was the property of the millionaires who controlled the United Shoe Machinery Company, and was a notable journalistic prostitute. Its editor, Robert Lincoln O'Brien, then 61 years old, was a South Boston Irishman who had worked his way through Harvard, and then somehow attracted the notice of Grover Cleveland, who had made him his personal secretary. On the conclusion of this employment he became Washington correspondent of the Boston *Transcript,* and later editor of the same. But in 1910 he transferred himself to the more congenial atmosphere of the Boston *Herald,* a stupid and vulgar sheet that printed very little serious news but was devoted mainly to reports of birthday parties, church raffles and other such puerile events in the meaner Boston suburbs. It was always extremely polite to Chase and his Puritan backers on the one hand, and to the Catholic hierarchy on the other. But when Judge Parmenter acquitted me, and I began to talk to the reporters about damage suits, O'Brien became alarmed, and on April 8 he printed a fourth editorial—this time impudently denying that the *Herald* had ever "expressed the opinion that the magazine was rightly suppressed"! That editorial even went to the length of admitting that there was "much verbal castigation of Mr. Chase and the Watch and Ward Society in Boston," and in conclusion it offered the smug observation that "the moral in this instance obviously is that a censor should be sure he has a case." A few days later the *Herald* printed a letter from a reader who took my side, and on April 15 it printed another (this time by a New Hampshire clergyman!) and on April 17 it concluded its somewhat devious *apologia* with the following:

> L. W. S., Waltham—If it is a fair question and your answer is printable, please tell me what you think of H. L. Mencken.
> Answer—Eminently fair and painlessly printable. Mr. Mencken is one of the most entertaining and stimulating of critics, with a cleverness that is all his own; occasionally he exhibits an unfairness that stirs the reader from amusement to annoyance; less frequently—far less frequently than in the case of his pathetically standardized, sophomoric chorus of imitators—he slips to the level of vulgarity and coarseness, and discards all the canons of good taste.

I doubted at the time and I doubt now that this inquiry from "L. W. S." was authentic; the chances are at least a hundred to one that it was manufactured in the *Herald* office. During the year following, as opposition to the Watch and Ward Society grew in Boston, and more and more influential persons began to show it, the *Herald* wobbled. On August 29, 1926 it was still subservient enough to the society to print a long defense of it by one Hugh Leamy, in which the Rev. Raymond Calkins, its president, was permitted to state a casuistical case for it. But by April, 1927, it was apparent that civilized opinion in Boston was overwhelmingly against it, and so the *Herald* flopped. In an editorial printed April 14 it addressed the wowsers as follows:

> Do not make us ridiculous. Do not imply to the world that those whom we elect to office have no comprehension of the intellectual freedom upon which the civilizations of the world have been built. Do not broadcast the idea that

we are children. Do not conclude that somebody must tell us what we may see, and read, and hear, and think.

The *Herald* assault, though it might have very well caused my conviction in Boston (and in England would certainly have got O'Brien punished for contempt of court), was less vicious than an editorial printed in the New York *Herald Tribune* of April 7, the morning of my acquittal. This was a thunderous broadside, not against "Hatrack" as obscene, but against "Hatrack" as sacrilegious, and it included a violent denunciation of me personally. The author, I was told, was one McPherson, a Scot who used to visit the *Smart Set* office trying to sell Nathan and me translations of banal French short stories. The war psychosis still raged in the office of the *Herald Tribune*, which had been described by Clement K. Shorter, in 1917 or thereabout, as "more English than we are English." McPherson, like many Scots, was even more English than the *Herald Tribune,* and so he had it in for one who had been notoriously pro-German during the war, and who lost no opportunity to denounce all Anglomaniacs as slimy and shabby fellows. Thus he described me: "He has nothing to offer in place of the familiar loyalties save a crude faith in the blood and iron of Teutonism. He is completely alien to America." A few days after this editorial appeared Alfred and Blanche Knopf encountered Helen Rogers Reid, wife of the chief proprietor of the *Herald Tribune* and its actual editor. She told them that she and her husband, coming up from Florida, had read McPherson's pious diatribe somewhere along the way, and were greatly distressed that it had got into the paper during their absence. But this must have been mainly only politeness, for the *Herald Tribune* showed no sign of repentance, but on the contrary printed two letters of approval from moral readers on April 9, and followed them with others during the week or two thereafter. Moreover, on April 22 it delivered a violent onslaught on Sinclair Lewis, who had lately stood up in a Kansas City church, declared his infidelity, and dared Jahveh to strike him dead. This performance, of course, was the ostensible provocation for the *Herald Tribune*'s attack, but its editorial writer (no doubt the pious McPherson again) took good care to link his infamy with mine.

The New York *Sun* was also hostile, but the *Times* and *World* were friendly, and the latter was notably so. Its first editorial on the case was written by James M. Cain, a Marylander and an old Baltimore *Sun* man. The New England papers, on the whole, were against Chase, even when they were not for me. In the South the reverse was true. I was, in those days, excessively unpopular down there, mainly on account of my essay, "The Sahara of the Bozart," first published in the *Smart Set* and then republished (with embellishments) in my "Prejudices: Second Series" (1920), but also on account of my reports of the Scopes trial in the Baltimore *Evening Sun* (July, 1925). The two Richmond papers, the *Times-Dispatch* and the *News-Leader,* belabored me lustily, and so did the Memphis *Commercial Appeal,* the Winston-Salem *Sentinel,* the Raleigh *News* and *Observer,* the Chattanooga *News,* the Knoxville *Sentinel,* the Atlanta *Journal,* and other such exponents of the Confederate *Kultur.* The Hon. Josephus Daniels, publisher of the Raleigh *News and Observer,* was not content to denounce me in his paper; he also gave out an interview calling me an enemy of "the home, the church, the law, and order." In it he confessed that he had not read "Hatrack." "I never," he said virtuously, "deliberately soil my soul." But there were also Southern editors who defended me, notably, Grover C. Hall of the Montgomery *Advertiser,* Duncan Aikman of the El Paso *Times,* and Julian and Julia Harris of the Columbus (Ga.) *Enquirer-Sun.* The Harrises, in particular, sustained my case with great vigor, and gave a great deal of space to it.

In the Middle West the newspapers were mainly against

me, for reasons analogous to those which caused so much hostility to me in the South. I had long derided both regions as benighted, and had given special attention to the degenerated forms of Protestant Christianity prevailing in them. The leaders of the attack were chiefly papers in relatively small places, for example, the Des Moines *Tribune*, the Lincoln (Neb.) *Journal*, the Wichita *Eagle* and *Beacon*, the Duluth *Herald*, the Omaha *Bee* and the Leavenworth *Times*, but some of the big city dailies also took a hand, for example, the Chicago *Post* and *Journal* and the Denver *Times*. The Hon. Henry J. Allen, then editor of the Wichita *Beacon*, printed a long and bitter tirade against me, accusing me of carrying on a war against every ideal cherished by the Christian people of the cow country. Spokesmen for the defense were rare in the Middle West, but there were a few, notably the Kansas City *Post* and the Omaha *World-Herald*. Further eastward were the Akron *Journal*, the Peoria *Transcript*, the Cleveland *Press*, the Indianapolis *Times*, the Columbus (O.) *Journal* and the Dubuque *Telegraph*. My old friend, E. W. Howe, of Atchison, Kansas, was against me, and said so frankly in *E. W. Howe's Monthly*. But we remained on good terms for all that.

My own paper, the Baltimore *Sun*, straddled. The *Evening Sun*, edited by Hamilton Owens (I had been officially attached to its staff since its establishment in 1910), was heartily for me, but the morning edition, edited by J. Haslup Adams, was for me only in part. Adams, who was a Liberal of the Manchester *Guardian* school, was also a Methodist, at least by birth, and his Methodism often collided with his Liberalism. That disharmony, in this case, caused him to argue on the one hand that "Hatrack" should not have been printed in a magazine "which, however high its intellectual and cultural level, does lie on the library tables of thousands of middle-class homes," and to insist violently on the other hand that the April issue should not have been suppressed. When I got back from my trial in Boston he upbraided me privately for printing the article, and was quite unable to see anything in it save a *chronique scandaleuse.* The very theme of it congealed his Wesleyan blood. But he remained a Liberal nevertheless, and in that character denounced the Boston wowsers with great vigor, and insisted that they had no right to attack any writing that was not "condemned in its entirety by the common judgment."

The general trend of the editorial comment, as I have said, was extremely hostile. Even those papers which criticized Chase and Donnelly commonly accused me of being animated by nothing better than a desire for free advertising. They had all suffered from censorship during the war, and very few of them had resisted. Now that I had done so in what appeared to them to be the grand manner, they resented, if only subconsciously, my appropriation of a job that they should, in honor, have taken on themselves. In other words, I was doing what they had been too timorous to do, and they had to ascribe an ignoble motive to me in order to justify themselves. Here I do not rely upon the Freudian quackery for support, but depend upon the letters that I received from a good many working newspaper men, telling me confidentially (and often indignantly) what was being said and done by their superiors. I was a free agent with a magazine of my own, and apparently having a hell of a good time; hence I was offensive to editors who had to step softly, with cowardly and tyrannical owners always at their heels. Moreover, many of these brethren were opposed in conscience to my whole scheme of things. In the average American town, including even most of the big cities, the editor of the leading local newspaper was almost always a Rotarian, and not infrequently he was also a member of one of the churches that I so constantly derided. In Richmond, Va., for example, Douglas S. Freeman, editor of the *News-Leader,* was superintendent of the largest Baptist Sunday-school, and in Oklahoma City Walter M. Harrison, managing editor of the Daily *Oklahoman* was pope of the Christian Scientists. The accumulated animosities of half a dozen years were now emptied upon me, and I appeared in most of the newspapers as a kind of racketeer. The fact that I was fighting a battle in which the whole press of the country had a stake was seldom mentioned.

But there were also papers which seemed to be honestly mistaken about my motives, and it occurred to me that it might be worth while to try to set them right. I accordingly prepared a statement headed "To the Friends of the *American Mercury,*" addressed both to them and to the subscribers to the magazine. It presented our case as I saw it, and included the judgments of Judge Parmenter and Morton. I prepared it during the busy days following the hearing before Donnelly. It was dated April 16, but it was not actually ready for circulation until after April 21. There was soon evidence that it was having a good effect. The Lynchburg (Va.) *News,* of which Senator Carter Glass was the owner, had denounced me violently on April 8 in an editorial headed "Barnum Advertises," but on May 8, after my statement had been digested, it apologized handsomely in an editorial at least five times as long. There were other signs of similar changes in view. We also sent out a reprint of Wood's article, "Keeping the Puritans Pure," with no comment, leaving it to tell its own story. Finally, I wrote a great many letters to editors who appeared, for one reason or another, to be susceptible to argumentation, and some of them were more friendly afterward.

Much to my surprise, we were supported by two religious weeklies, the *Congregationalist* of Chicago and the *Christian Leader* of Richmond, Va. The *Congregationalist,* on April 8, deplored "Hatrack" as "an unsavory thing" that was "no credit to the *American Mercury,*" but spoke of the maga-

zine as having "admirable" as well as "objectionable" qualities. It went on: "We have seen nothing in it that warrants
legal efforts to prevent its sale. Even this mean-spirited
sketch called 'Hatrack' has a certain sociological value." "Is
the church going to gain in prestige, respect and influence,"
asked the editor, "by appealing to the police in a situation
that she ought to be meeting by the strength and power
of her own witness?" This editorial was widely quoted in
the newspapers, and it greatly upset Chase and his fellow
wowsers of the Watch and Ward Society. The support of
the *Christian Leader* was even more astonishing, for it was
a Methodist paper, edited by a clergyman of that sect. "In
our opinion," he said in his issue of April 17, "the Boston
judge [Parmenter] was right. The article is not impure or
suggestive. . . . There can only be mingled chagrin and
amusement over the incident, and admiration for Mr.
Mencken for sticking to his guns and fighting the battle of
liberty." This editorial caused a sensation among the Methodists, and many of them wrote to the editor, denouncing
him. But he refused to change his tune. The other Methodist
weeklies, when they gave any space to the business at all,
were implacably hostile. The *Voice*, monthly organ of the
M. E. Board of Temperance, Prohibition and Public Morals
at Washington, linked me with Earl Carroll, the bawdy
theatrical manager, and denounced the *American Mercury*
as "one of the vilest literary publications in America."

Some of the newspapers added to our troubles inadver-
tently, by inquiring of the wowsers of their towns whether
action was to be taken against the April issue locally. These
naïve suggestions provoked a number of efforts at suppression, and stirred up police chiefs and district attorneys eager
for easy publicity. The first prosecuting attorney to get
national attention was Harry F. Hittle at Lansing, Mich.,
who ordered the April issue removed from the news-stands
of Ingham county on April 8. "The story," he announced,

"clearly violates the Michigan statute prohibiting publication of 'deeds of lust or crime,' and another statute barring publications tending to corrupt the morals of the young." This Hittle had got some attention several months before by ordering the Lansing newsdealers to stop selling fifteen other magazines. The dealers obeyed him promptly, and so the matter never got into the courts. The Attorney-General of Michigan refused to be associated with the attack on the *American Mercury*, but Hittle kept on with it so long as it yielded any publicity. On April 10 he gave a statement to the Lansing State *Journal* which included the following:

> The article "Hatrack" is . . . indecent and sacrilegious in its intimation that Christian cemeteries are habitually used for immoral purposes. . . . I am a regular reader of the *Atlantic Monthly.* This is a conservative publication, but I derive much enjoyment from its pages.

In North Carolina the newspapers unearthed a State statute which forbade the sale of any magazine that had been barred from the mails. This curious law, approved August 21, 1924, had been introduced in the Legislature by Representative Frank D. Grist, who was also a member of the legislative committee of the American Legion. It was aimed mainly at subversive publications, many of which had been barred from the mails between 1917 and 1924, but it was very wide in scope, and its title called it "An Act to Prevent the Sale and Distribution of Obscene Literature." It deserves to be cited in full:

> It shall be unlawful for any news-agent, newsdealer, bookseller, or any other person, firm or corporation to offer for sale, sell or cause to be circulated within the State of North Carolina any magazine, periodical or other publication which is now or may hereafter be excluded from the United States mails.

It shall be unlawful for any person, firm or corporation to offer for sale, sell or give to any person under the age of twenty-one any such magazine, periodical, or any other publication which is now or may hereafter be excluded from the United States mails.

That this act shall not be construed to in any way conflict with or abridge the freedom of the press, and shall in no way affect any publication which is permitted to be sent through the United States mails.

That any person, firm or corporation violating any of the provisions of this act shall be guilty of a misdemeanor.

The Raleigh correspondent of the Winston-Salem *Sentinel,* writing on April 10, reported that there was talk in Raleigh of inviting me to North Carolina to test this singular law. No such invitation was ever received, and if it had come in I'd have been forced to decline, for we had enough action on other fronts to keep me busy, and I was not much interested in what went on in North Carolina. As a matter of fact, the April issue seems to have been unmolested in the State, though Grist the legislator went on a tour of the newsstands, snooping for it, and it was denounced by nearly all the local newspapers, including the ostensibly Liberal Greensboro *News.* While all this was going on it was available to any reader at the State Library in Raleigh.

The newspapers, between the end of March and the middle of April, were full of dispatches from towns, East, West, North and South, reporting either local action against us, or the lack of such action. Most of the Massachusetts towns outside Boston refused to obey Chase's mandate, and in New Bedford the leading bookseller, Robert C. Saltmarsh, denounced him publicly. But Worcester, Fall River and Pittsfield finally yielded. In Waterbury, Conn., the head of the Bronson Library, H. Lindsey Brown, first put the April issue on his reserve list, and then removed it from circulation altogether. In Poughkeepsie, N.Y., the local district attorney, Allen S. Reynolds, was incited by the Law Enforcement League, headed by the Rev. William Bancroft Hill, to ban the magazine, but it continued on file at the Adriance Memorial Library there. In Memphis, Tenn., the mayor, Rowlett Paine, denounced it, but refused to ban it, saying that he didn't believe "it could be classed as lewd." So far as we could make out at the time the only places in the United States where its sale was actually forbidden, outside New England, were Lansing, Mich. and Poughkeepsie. But in many towns, large and small, it was removed from the shelves of the local libraries, sometimes on the ground that it was too strong meat for general consumption, but more often on the ground that the demand for it was so great as to constitute a nuisance. Not a few libraries announced that their copies had been stolen. On April 6 the New York *Herald*'s Paris edition reported that the April issue had been removed from the American Library there, but this seemed incredible and turned out to be untrue.

The evangelical clergy naturally made the most of the opportunity the attempt to suppress the magazine afforded, and many of them launched into pious attacks upon it and me. At the New York East Conference of the Methodist Episcopal Church, held in Brooklyn on April 9, three of the pastors present were heard on the subject, and in Youngstown, O., on April 12, the Rev. W. E. Hammacker preached a sermon in Trinity M. E. Church denouncing the article on the Methodists in the April issue, and calling "Hatrack" "a vice report written by a man who could put a chuckle into it." In Boston itself the Rev. A. Z. Conrad, pastor of the Park Street Church, in front of which I had sold the magazine to Chase, told his congregation on April 11 that I was "lost to the high ideals of life." At Durham, N.C., the Rev. H. E. Spence, a professor in the department of religious education at Duke University, advised the congregation of Duke Memorial Methodist Church that the *Ameri-*

can Mercury was biased and wicked, and at New Haven, Conn., the Rev. Ralph W. Stockman, pastor of the Madison Avenue Methodist Episcopal Church, New York City, told the church-goers among the faculty and student body of Yale that there was "a vast difference between Mencken selling his forbidden *Mercury* on Boston Common and James Otis arguing against the unjust writs of assistance." In Denver the Rev. William O'Ryan, of St. Leo's Catholic Church, gave the *Express* an interview in which he called "Hatrack" unredeemed dirt, an open sewer, without even the iridescent scum that sometimes half invites and half excuses a glance." It did not deserve, he opined, "the publicity of a verdict of condemnation"; it was "sheer lubricity, to be silently shunned." But two other Denver clergymen, the Rev. David H. Fourse of the Seventeenth Avenue Community Church, and the Rev. Harold H. Niles of the First Universalist Church, refused to go along with Father O'Ryan. Both, on the contrary, defended the *American Mercury.* So did the Rev. Fred Winslow Adams of Trinity Methodist Church, Springfield, Mass., who gave his flock to understand that the Boston comstocks were idiots. So, also, did the Rev. J. V. Moldenhower, of Westminster Presbyterian Church, Albany, N.Y., who advised the clergy at a Troy conference of Methodists which he addressed as a guest speaker, to read the magazine; and the Rev. Charles J. Dutton, of the First Unitarian Church, Erie, Pa., who gave the Erie *Times* an interview saying that my arrest was "absolutely absurd and uncalled for"; and the Rev. John Emerson Roberts, of the Church of This World, Kansas City, who told his congregation that "Hatrack" was not obscene, and described me as one who "sees with keenness and speaks without fear"; and the Rev. W. T. McElveen, of Plymouth Congregational Church, St. Paul, Minn., who denounced all moral reformers as Pharisees. After my acquittal I received a number of letters of congratulation from clergymen, including Bishop Charles

Fiske, of the Protestant Episcopal diocese of Central New York, and the Rev. Joseph J. Ayd, S.J., then of Georgetown University, Washington.

The reaction of the *American Mercury's* subscribers was, on the whole, extremely favorable to us, and we received very few cancellations. Letters came in from a great many of them. The lawyers appeared to be generally for us, and offers of legal help came from a dozen or more. Zechariah Chafee, Jr., professor of law in the Harvard Law School, presented our case to his class in equity in June, 1926, and asked its members to consider the principles of law involved. "Do not limit your discussion," he instructed them, "to one possible ground for relief, if more than one is reasonably conceivable." The *Virginia Law Register* for May printed an editorial headed "Still More Censorship: The Case of H. L. Mencken," in which Chase and Donnelly were both handled very realistically. The literati showed relatively little interest in the case: I was not popular in that quarter, partly on account of my book reviews and partly because I had given over the *American Mercury* mainly to new writers, and excluded most of the established performers. George Ade was a notable exception: he sent me a hearty letter on April 20, though I had but lately declined one of his articles. Other letters came from Henry S. Canby, Edwin Björkman, James M. Cain, Daniel Gregory Mason and Barrett H. Clark. Gamaliel Bradford, on receiving "To the Friends of the *American Mercury*," sent a qualified approval, saying he was glad I had challenged the "stupid and dangerous" methods of the Watch and Ward Society, but calling "Hatrack" unprofitable and thoroughly objectionable in tone." Lieut.-Col. Fielding H. Garrison, of the Army Medical Corps, who had contributed an article on William S. Halsted, the surgeon, to the April issue, was similarly on the fence. He wrote to me on April 8, offering formal congratulations but calling "Hatrack" "trite, naif, *vieux jeu* and unsophisticated" and saying that he was "a little nettled over proximity to it." Four days later he sent me a second letter, saying, "the article affected me like the odor of a country privy."

At the time of my arrest Sinclair Lewis was in Kansas City gathering material for "Elmer Gantry." In this business he had the help of the Rev. L. M. Birkhead, pastor of All Souls' Unitarian Church, better known as the Liberal Center. I had met Birkhead at Dayton, Tenn., during the Scopes trial, and had advised Lewis to consult him. On April 6 Lewis sent me a friendly telegram, and on April 7, the day of my acquittal, he followed it with a characteristic letter of congratulations. Two days later he gave an interview to one of the Kansas City papers, supporting me royally, and parts of it were sent out that night by the Associated Press. "Elmer Gantry," which was dedicated to me, was published early in 1927, and caused an immediate uproar. The Boston comstocks, by that time, had become excessively cautious, but a new district attorney of Suffolk county, William J. Foley by name, was willing to plunge in where they feared to tread, and on April 13 he ordered the local booksellers to cease selling "Elmer Gantry." The Boston Booksellers' Committee, headed by the egregious Fuller, protested that it had a gentleman's agreement with the district attorney's office providing that the latter should not act save on the motion of the Watch and Ward Society. But Foley refused to honor this agreement, which had been made by his predecessor, Thomas C. O'Brien, to whom he was very hostile. He was encouraged in his stand by the Boston *Pilot,* the archdiocesan organ of Cardinal William H. O'Connell. The following other novels were banned by Foley at the same time: "The Plastic Age," by Percy Marks; "The Hard-Boiled Virgin," by Frances Newman; "The Rebel Bird," by Diana Patrick; "The Butcher Shop," by Jean Devanny; "The Ancient Hunger," by Edwin Granberry; "Antennae," by Hulbert Footner; "The Marriage Bed," by Ernest Pascal; "The Beadle," by Pauline Smith; and

"As It Was," by H. T. In a little while the following were added to the list: "The World of William Clissold," by H. G. Wells; "Little Pitchers," by Isa Glenn; "The Sun Also Rises," by Ernest Hemingway; "Doomsday," by Warwick Deeping; and "An American Tragedy," by Theodore Dreiser. When the ban on "Elmer Gantry" was announced the Boston *Herald* had the effrontery to telegraph to me, asking what I thought of it. I replied as follows on April 12, 1927:

> My sincere congratulations to the *Herald* and to its allies of the Watch and Ward Society. Its long and heroic campaign to purge Massachusetts of books and reduce the whole population to the intellectual level of its own editorial writers is bearing gorgeous fruit. The next step must be the suppression of the Harvard University. It is more dangerous to the moron *Kultur* than a dozen "Elmer Gantrys." Let its faculty and students come down to the Maryland Free State.

The *Herald* did not print this telegram, but I gave it to the Associated Press, and it was published elsewhere. I never received any reply to it.

As I have hitherto recorded, the Chamber of Commerce of the town of Farmington, Mo., the scene of "Hatrack," adopted a resolution on April 8, 1926, asking Postmaster General New to bar the April issue from the mails. No copy of it had gone to Farmington in the regular course: the first one seen there was shown to the local dignitaries by an exploring newspaper correspondent from St. Louis—Marquis W. Childs of the United Press. The ensuing pother was fomented by the Rev. J. F. Jarnigan, a Methodist clergyman. He induced the Chamber of Commerce to call a meeting to denounce the article. At that meeting the chairman began to read it, but was halted by M. T. Casey, the town banker, who exclaimed: "Stop reading that! We should not listen to such an immoral recital!" No one in Farmington ventured to deny the essential truth of Asbury's account of poor Hatrack. In fact, the mayor admitted to Childs that it was substantially accurate. What he complained of, he said, was "the slur cast upon all the other women of the town." But these other women, of course, were not actually mentioned. "I am in favor," said the Rev. Mr. Jarnigan, "of having the magazine barred forever from this country." Childs found that Hatrack was still living in a nearby village called Flat River. On his return to St. Louis on April 9 he telegraphed to me as follows:

It occurred to me that perhaps you would like for immediate use an account of Hatrack's subsequent history. It is a record of hypocrisy and cruelty which far exceeds anything told by Asbury. From the humanitarian point of view it seems that I can in no way harm the woman, as Farmington has done everything in that direction that it is possible to do, and it might reveal some of the cruelty and savagery of small town morality now, when a pathetic public attention is directed upon the entire matter. . . . I have Hatrack's history from a former townsman, a most reliable and honest person.

I replied that I hesitated to give the poor wretch another bath of publicity, and on April 15 Childs wrote to me as follows:

On more sober reflection, and before I had your letter, I came to the same opinion: that Hatrack or some of her numerous progeny might suffer from further notice. I wired you just after I had heard her story, with all the cruelty and barbarism that it implies. . . .

The woman who is indisputably Hatrack has given rise to an illegitimate line in Farmington. Not only are half a dozen of her illegitimate offspring living there, but an imbecile daughter of thirty has two or three children of her own whose paternity is unknown. This daughter . . . decks her bastards out in the clothing which some good Christian soul has condescended to hand down, and tramps the middle of the town to church each Sunday—sometimes to one church and sometimes to another. She is accorded slightly more charity; "she is not quite right" it is whispered. Hatrack has abandoned the fight for the Christian life and gone to Flat River, a mining town, where her talents are more appreciated. I don't think that either Hatrack or her daughter could be injured by anything said about them; they are quite beyond that. But there is a son who seems to embody all the elements of genuine tragedy: a rather fine-looking youngster of nineteen, an athlete in the high-school, and now at a junior college in Flat River, and, as far as I could gather, a fine, sensitive person.

Childs offered to make affidavit to what he had discovered in Farmington, for possible use in our legal proceedings, and to get a supporting affidavit from a Farmington young man, but the chance to use this material never offered, and so we did not ask for it. At the invitation of the United Press, Asbury wrote a counterblast to Farmington's indignant complaint, saying, among other things, that its time for indignation "was twenty years ago, when the poor creature yearned for decent human companionship." I was also asked to say something on the subject, and accordingly gave the United Press the following: "These worthy Christians simply prove Mr. Asbury's case. My suggestion is that they hang all the town evangelists and begin to read the Sermon on the Mount." On May 12 Paul Palmer, then on the staff of the St. Louis *Post-Dispatch,* sent me some Farmington photographs—one showing the Catholic cemetery in which Hatrack entertained her Protestant clients, and another showing the Masonic cemetery to which she took Catholics. I received a number of letters from readers who insisted that Hatrack was falsely ascribed to Farmington—that she had really infested villages with which they were familiar, some in the Middle West but others in the East. Under date of "A Western Kansas Town, April 10" I received a letter from one subscribing herself "A Hatrack." She said that she recognized the picture that Asbury had drawn, and concluded sadly: "Doubtless few will change their attitudes toward Hatracks through the audacity of your article." On April 10 the International News Service sent out the following from New Bedford, Mass.: "Indignant over cemetery petters who make love on the tombstones at Rural Cemetery, Mrs. Alex Tripp, who lives a few yards from the graveyard, has complained to the police."

Boston (Mass.)
Advertiser

Youngstown (O.)
Telegram

Washington (D.C.)
Times

Chase Illegally Barred Mercury, Says U. S. Court

Publisher Mencken Will Now Sue Watch and Ward for $50,000

The American Mercury, which scored a victory over J. Frank Chase and the Watch and Ward Society in the Federal District Court yesterday, is now prepared to go ahead with its efforts to collect damages for suppression of the sale of the April issue of the magazine containing the famous "Hatrack" article.

The amount of damage has been tentatively set at $50,000 by the magazine.

The court victory yesterday included an opinion by Judge Morton that Chase and the Watch and Ward have been acting illegally and a temporary injunction restraining the society and its agent from interfering with the magazine further by intimidation.

The court said it is not legal to warn magazine and book distributors not to sell or distribute, under pain of prosecution, any book or article of which the society disapproves.

J. Frank Chase

FAIL TO GET EXTRA COPIES OF MERCURY

Magazine Can't Be Purchased Despite Lifting Of Ban

Altho the ban on the sale of the American Mercury was lifted by a court order Wednesday, the April issue wasn't to be purchased in Youngstown today.

This issue, in which appeared "Hatrack" which resulted in the number being barred the use of the mails, has been completely sold out here and dealers aren't expecting any more.

In restraining the Boston Watch and Ward society from interfering with the sale of Mercury, the judge said the organization "has no right to impose its opinion on the book and magazine trade by threats of prosecution if its views are not accepted."

* * *

By United Press

WASHINGTON, April 15.—Horace J. Donnelly, solicitor of the postoffice department today denied an appeal made by H. J. Mencken, publisher, to re-open the United States mails for the April issue of the Mercury magazine.

MENCKEN WARS ON P. O. BAN

H. L. Mencken, editor of American Mercury, today appealed to the Postoffice Department to rescind its order barring from the mails the April issue because it contained the story "Hatrack," dealing with prostitution in a small Western town.

In its order, the department has overstepped the law barring publications of indecent character, Arthur Garfield Hayes, attorney for Mencken, told H. J. Donnelly, solicitor of the Postoffice.

Donnelly became angered over suggestions that the Postoffice barred the magazine because of attempts of the Watch and Ward society to ban the publication from sale in Boston.

Hayes argued that the article was not indecent because it appealed to the mind, not the emotions.

Washington (D.C.) Times

MENCKEN FAILS TO HAVE MAGAZINE BAN LIFTED

H. L. Mencken apparently failed today in his appeal to the Postoffice Department to restore mailing privileges to the April number of the American Mercury, which was barred because of "Hatrack," a story.

No change in the Postoffice Department's ruling was announced by Solicitor Donnelly at the close of a hearing given the editor, and it was indicated there would be none.

Mencken said he feared his enemies would try to have the May issue barred, and Donnelly told him to submit it to the postmaster at Camden, N. J., for an opinion.

IX

OUR appeal to the Federal District Court for Southern New York against the Postoffice order barring the April issue from the mails was filed on April 28, just short of two weeks after the buffoonish hearing in Washington. It took Hays and his associates that long to look up the pertinent precedents, and prepare the bill of complaint. An order to show cause was signed the same day by Judge Thomas D. Thacher, and the hearing was set for May 4. The government asked for a postponement until May 11, and this was granted. Its effect was to transfer the trial of the case from Judge Thacher to Judge Julian W. Mack, a circuit judge of the Seventh Circuit, temporarily assigned to the District Court in New York to help clear off a congested docket. The government was represented by Donnelly, Kelly, O'Brien and Thomas J. Crawford, an assistant to Emory R. Buckner, the Federal district attorney at New York.

The proceedings were brief. Hays presented an affidavit by me setting forth the facts already recited in this chronicle, and including "To the Friends of the *American Mercury*" as an appendix, and another by Asbury deposing that "Hatrack" was "truth and not fiction," and that his "purpose was not to appeal to or arouse sexual or lewd thoughts." The government, in its turn, presented affidavits by Donnelly, Kiely, New, and a Postoffice inspector named Dana F. Angier, hitherto unheard of in the case. The Angier affidavit, of which we had had no previous notice whatever, introduced an entirely new charge, to wit, that a quarter-page advertisement of Harry F. Marks bookshop in New York, printed in the April issue, offered for sale Brantome's "Lives of Fair and Gallant Ladies," which had been "previously ruled by the Department to be obscene and unmailable under the provisions of Section 470 of the current Postal Laws and Regulations (Sec. 211, U.S.C.C.)." Angier swore that, under the name of James B. Waterman, he had sent Marks $17.50 for a copy of this work, and that with it he had received a catalogue offering various other wicked books, including the Decameron of Boccaccio, the works of Rabelais, the memoirs of Casanova, the essays of Montaigne, and the Heptameron of Margaret of Navarre, not to mention the Enfield Edition of Charles Lamb, and Walton's "Compleat Angler"! This Marks advertisement had been appearing in a dozen other magazines, including *Harper's*, always without challenge. There was absolutely nothing indecent on its face, and it offered only four books—the Brantome, "The Compleat Angler," the memoirs of Harriet Wilson, and Burton's "Arabian Nights"—all of which were on common sale in New York and the other larger cities of the country. We had never received any notice that Brantome was forbidden in the mails, and the fact was apparently unknown to other magazine publishers. We had always been very careful about the advertising admitted to the *American Mercury*, and whenever the advertising manager, Bachman, or his assistant in charge of book advertising, Louis N. Brockway, were in doubt they were in the habit of consulting me. But they had not consulted me about the Marks advertisement, for it appeared to be quite harmless.

In Kiely's affidavit, drawn up by Donnelly, there was another astonishing novelty. This was the contention, made in all solemnity, that we were not entitled to relief because the April issue was already through the mails—in other words, that the Postoffice could not be restrained from inflicting upon us an injury that could have no conceivable public utility, even assuming "Hatrack" to be obscene, and was thus purely punitive and malicious! I quote:

> The court's attention is respectfully invited to the fact that nowhere in the moving affidavit or in the bill of complaint is there any statement or allegation that there are any copies of the said April, 1926, issue of the said publication in the possession of the complainant or of anyone else which have been refused the privileges of the mails by virtue of the decision of the Postoffice Department hereinabove referred to. Quite the contrary appears to be true. In the affidavit in support of the motion and in the bill of complaint it is alleged that practically the whole of the April, 1926, edition of said publication had been mailed and delivered before April 5, 1926, and on page 2 of Exhibit 1 attached to and made a part of the moving affidavit of Henry L. Mencken, the editor of the said magazine, in a statement "To the Friends of the *American Mercury,*" it is admitted that the whole of the said edition had been mailed and delivered before April 5, 1926, save for a few copies held for stock, and it is further admitted in said statement that "the question of mailability of the number was purely academic."

This preposterous argument was to be accepted gravely, a year later, by a Circuit Court of Appeals, but Judge Mack dismissed it without ceremony. As I have said, I was not present at the hearing, but remained in Baltimore. During the early afternoon I received the following telegram from Hays:

> We knocked them again in injunction granted by Judge Mack. Government caught on their own spike, having asked for adjournment of week, which brought case before Judge Mack. "Hatrack" has gone to the rear. Brantome takes front seat. On page xxxiii is an ad of bookshop where Brantome's works can be secured. Failing with "Hatrack," government argument turned to "Clinical Notes." Failing with this, they tried the advertisement. The three Postoffice solicitors were in court, and seemed aggrieved.

Later in the day Hays prepared the following record of the proceedings and gave it to the newspapers:

> Argument took place this morning before Judge Julian W. Mack on the motion brought by the *American Mercury* to enjoin the Postoffice Department from preventing the circulation through the mails of the April number of the *American Mercury*. The Postoffice appeared by Thomas J. Crawford of Mr. Buckner's staff. The *Mercury* appeared by Arthur Garfield Hays.
>
> The injunction was granted, Judge Mack saying that he found nothing in the magazine that was obscene or indecent in the purview of the law. He stated that the article "Hatrack" might excite disgust at certain conditions and that this might have a healthy influence. The Government argued that since the *Mercury* claimed that practically all of the April edition had been mailed in the early part of March and April, the question was academic. The Court held that if there was only one copy that the *Mercury* was forbidden to mail, they were entitled to an injunction, if the Postmaster General was wrong. The Court further pointed out that any individual was in danger of indictment if he mailed his copy.
>
> The Government further contended that the question in-

volved was one committed by Congress to the discretion of the Postoffice Department. On this proposition there was no doubt unless the action of the Postoffice Department was arbitrary and without foundation. Judge Mack said that if the question before him was one of whether or not the article violated the law, he would not even have a momentary hesitation. The Government had made the argument that the *Mercury* had had a fair hearing because after it was barred from the mails, Mr. Mencken and Mr. Hays were given an opportunity to appear in Washington and a brief was submitted, to which the solicitors of the Postoffice Department had given consideration. They admitted that the same men who had held the article unmailable had passed on the matter the second time and that they adhered to their original ruling.

In court, however, the Government claimed that in addition to "Hatrack," they found objection to "Clinical Notes," and that if this would not do, they also objected to the advertisement on page xxxiii of the ads, wherein an advertiser, the Harry F. Marks Bookshop, had drawn attention to Brantome's "Lives of Fair and Gallant Ladies," a book which they claimed was in violation of the law. They pointed out that the advertising of an obscene book was a violation of the statute. In answer to this, Mr. Hays stated that he was very pleased that the Postoffice Department had shown its hand. It was apparent that they were out to "get" the *Mercury*.

"The busy-bodies and snoopers of Boston," said Mr. Hays, "failing on the 'Hatrack' article, turned to 'Clinical Notes,' about which Judge Parmenter said, 'It was not seriously urged that this article violated the statute.' Now the Postoffice Department goes one step further in its endeavor to 'get' the *Mercury* and in spite of its pretenses of giving a fair trial, it has had one of its hirelings go through the magazine with a magnifying glass to discover something about which no one had made any objection, but which might support the position taken for an entirely different reason. This throws some light upon the desire of the Postoffice

Department not to ban the *Mercury* because of a particular article but to ban the *Mercury* for any reason whatever."

The Court held that this was an afterthought, that the Brantome books had not theretofore been made an issue, and that they were works originally published in the Seventeenth Century, bringing them within the definition of classics.

As to the *Mercury* in general, Judge Mack said in substance, that he was a subscriber, that he had read "Hatrack," that there was nothing in the article that could arouse the sexual passions of anybody but a degenerate, that no normal human being could possibly be morally affected by it, that if the test of literature was its effect upon degenerates, almost anything might be banned. On the bench Judge Mack read "Clinical Notes" and said he found nothing therein that was objectionable. He stated that perhaps he was extreme in his views of the freedom of the press, but that in his opinion the action of the Postoffice Department was without foundation.

"Therefore," said Judge Mack, "I will grant the injunction."

The text of the order was as follows:

ORDERED, ADJUDGED AND DECREED that the motion for the injunction *pendende lite* herein be and the same hereby is granted, and the said defendants, their agents, servants and employees are hereby restrained and enjoined from treating the April, 1926 issue of said magazine known as the *American Mercury* as nonmailable matter, and the said defendants, their agents, servants and employees are commanded forthwith to transmit said issue of said magazine known as the *American Mercury* through the mails from the New York Postoffice and any other postoffice maintained by the United States Government in the usual way without further delay.

On June 4 the government filed an assignment of errors,

and on July 1 a notice of appeal. The hearing on the appeal was set by Judge John R. Hazel of the Federal District Court for July 31, but it was not until November 9 that the case got on the calendar of the Circuit Court of appeals, and not until May, 1927, that it was heard.

Donnelly's calculated unfairness in all these proceedings—first offering the Boston comstocks aid and comfort in defeat by assaulting us behind our backs, then sitting as judge in our appeal against his action, and then, before Judge Mack, suddenly shifting his attack from "Hatrack," the original *casus belli*, to the Marks advertisement, which had never been mentioned before—these disingenuous manoeuvres were extremely irritating, and I was certainly not mollified by the argument he offered to Judge Mack—that we were entitled to no relief against him because his whole onslaught was *ex post facto* and without effect. It had had, in fact, some very damaging effects, and more were still flowing out of it. It had lost us some advertising, it had brought down upon us a furious barrage of newspaper abuse and misrepresentation, it had encouraged comstocks everywhere to imitate Chase, and it had cost us a great deal of money. The *American Mercury*, at that time, was but little more than two years old, and if it came to be thought of as a sensational and pornographic magazine it might well be ruined. I had put a great deal of hard work into it, and was reasonably proud of the success that it had made, and of the high character of its cliéntèle. Nathan, from the start, had given me very little help, for it quickly appeared that he was completely ignorant of most of the matters it presumed to deal with: his mind was focused on New York, and especially on Broadway. I therefore had to drop him, and taken on the whole job myself, with only such help as I could get from Angoff, who was a young man but a few years out of college, and hence lacking in experience and judgment. He was diligent and intelligent, but I simply could not trust him to track down and contract for articles and prepare them for publication. I was thus very hard worked, and it seemed intolerable that all my effort should now be set at naught by such frauds as Donnelly and Chase.

Beside, there was the danger to my own fortunes to think of. I had accumulated, through my writings during the war and afterward, a large crop of bitter enemies, and some of them were extremely enterprising. They now had, thanks to the two wowsers, a good stick to beat me with, and they employed it with much industry. I could, of course, strike back, both in the *American Mercury* and elsewhere, but numbers were against me, and I could count on very little help from others. Thus I knew that I had a long and difficult fight ahead, and that I could win it only by taking and maintaining a vigorous offensive. Many papers, in the course of the "Hatrack" uproar, had libelled me grossly and obviously, and I toyed for a while with the idea of suing some of them. But this plan was quickly abandoned, for I had always made it my policy to offer no objection to anything written about me, however inaccurate, and I didn't want to change that policy now. Finally, it occurred to me that it might be a good scheme to use Judge Mack's decision as ground for filing charges against Donnelly with New, the Postmaster General. To be sure, New's decision could run only one way, but the hearings would attract attention, and might offer me the chance to plaster Donnelly in the grand manner, and make him an object of general ridicule, and even of general detestation. Moreover, they would give me the pleasant satisfaction of carrying the war into the enemy's camp. I accordingly wrote to Hays on May 22, asking him if he approved. He replied as follows on May 24:

> I think your idea . . . is a good one. I don't think we will get anywhere if the basis is merely a mistake in the law, and I am hopeful you have other grounds. The mere filing

of charges, however, would undoubtedly upset Donnelly considerably.

I accordingly drew up a petition to New, asking for a public hearing and demanding that, in case I should prove my charges, Donnelly should be "dismissed from the service of the Postoffice Department." This I sent to Hays on May 27, along with two memoranda showing that, in dealing with cancer quacks and other such dangerous frauds, the Postoffice was always careful to give every accused person what amounted to a public trial, with the right to counsel. The material for the latter I obtained by a diligent study of the reports of various Postmasters-General, and of the files of the *Journal of the American Medical Association.* Hays wrote to me on May 28, advising me that "it would be better tactics to wait until the government appeals." "I doubt very much," he continued, "if action would be taken during an appeal. The appeal itself will not come up until next Fall. At the same time, I want you to consider the question whether, if the government actually takes an appeal, it might not be well, for psychological purposes, to file the petition at that time." He suggested two small changes in the text, and added that it might be well to attempt a collection of other April, 1926, magazines, to show that many of them contained matter much more inflammatory than "Hatrack." They would be useful, he said, in proving discrimination against the *American Mercury.* "In fact," he concluded, "I think this should be almost the basis of our position." But when, on July 1, the government filed its notice of appeal Hays was on a trip abroad, and nothing was done about my petition. He did not return until September 1. By that time it was necessary to begin preparations for trying the appeal, and my petition got itself forgotten, to be recalled no more until the present moment. I still believe that filing it would have been excellent tactics.

Very few newspapers were friendly to Donnelly, for he was always harassing them about reports of lotteries and other such vexatious trivialities, and many that had been belaboring me violently would have fallen upon him, once he was under attack, with just as much vigor.

One of my good friends in those days was Senator James A. Reed of Missouri, then a very powerful figure in the Senate. He had been attracted by my essay, "Puritanism as a Literary Force," printed in my "Book of Prefaces" (1917), and we had been in frequent correspondence. When the *American Mercury* was set up I asked him to do an article for it, and he responded with "The Pestilence of Fanaticism," published in May, 1925. When I went to Washington for the burlesque hearing before Donnelly I missed seeing Reed, but he wrote to me on April 24, and a little while later I went to Washington again, and had a session with him. He was very wrathy over Donnelly's proceedings, and proposed to go to his friend New, a former colleague in the Senate, and, as he said, "give him a hell of a good dressing-down." I dissuaded him from this, saying that we wanted to fight the matter out in the open, and feared that any effort to intimidate New would be bad tactics. Reed, of course, was a Democrat and New was a Republican, but Reed was much the more intelligent and influential, and New would be loath to get into a row with him. Reed replied that he proposed to act, not as a Senator but as our legal adviser, but I still declined. He used to say afterward that I was the only person in the United States who had ever refused his offer of free legal services. He was a very successful lawyer, and had figured in many important cases. Moreover, he was then one of the dominant personalities of the Senate, and very few of his colleagues were willing to stand up to him in debate. A bit later on Paul Y. Anderson, of the Washington bureau of the St. Louis *Post-Dispatch*, proposed to him that he introduce a bill setting up a quasi-judicial tribunal to determine the mailability of publications, thus destroying Donnelly's arbitrary power. Reed was willing, but in view of our greater familiarity with the facts, suggested that Hays draw up the bill. He also asked Anderson to prepare a written statement of what had occurred at the grotesque hearing before Donnelly. But Anderson left soon afterward for a trip to the West and Hays was presently on his way to Europe, so nothing was ever done. In fact, before anything could have been done Congress was ready for adjournment.

In the House of Representatives the only member who showed any interest in the case was Victor L. Berger of Wisconsin, the lone Socialist. On April 27, the day before we appealed to the Federal District Court in New York against Donnelly, he made a speech in the House attacking the Post-office censorship and all other such impediments to free speech and a free press. The relevant parts follow:

And then there is the recent case of the *American Mercury*, a monthly magazine . . . edited by America's foremost critic, Henry L. Mencken. Because it published a story which some prudes thought was immoral, but which many people believed was in reality a highly moral lesson showing up the hypocrisy of some of the yokel towns of the Middle West, its sale was forbidden. When a judge in Boston freed the magazine the Postmaster-General forbade its circulation.

Now, with all due respect to the Postmaster-General, I do not believe that he is an absolute judge of either good literature or good morals. He ought therefore to be deprived of the autocratic power that he has of ruining any publication at random if he so chooses. The Postmaster-General, like any other mortal, should be compelled to go to the courts and prove his case against the publication before he could stop its circulation. I would give no man living the unlimited censorship over free speech and over free press. . . .

Mr. Speaker, have the American people lost their faith in democratic institutions? There seems to be less concern here about the loss of civil liberty than in any Western European country. There is surely less resistance against Federal, State and local tyranny. We have truly become a docile people.

Meanwhile, I struggled with the immense correspondence that the case had produced, and prepared statements for various friendly newspapers.

X

J UDGE Morton's injunction against the Watch and Ward Society gave the Boston comstocks a severe shock, and even before it was followed by Judge Mack's injunction against the Postoffice they began to show signs of yearning to be rid of the *American Mercury* case. The preponderance of literate opinion in Boston was strongly against them, and many Bostonians of influence were indignant over the evil advertising that they had given the town—not for the first time, by any means, nor for the tenth. By the middle of April we were hearing reports that some of the supporters of the society were withdrawing their support, and that Chase was very much worried. We heard, too, that he was in great fear lest we proceed to sue him for damages, and the society likewise. There was a report in the Boston morning newspapers of April 21 which showed the way the wind was blowing. It was to the effect that Herbert A. Wilson, the commissioner of police, had instructed Superintendent Michael H. Crowley to give Chase no more aid without first submitting all the facts to him (Wilson) and waiting for his specific instructions. "The order was brought about," said the Boston *Globe*, "through the arrest a few weeks ago, in the vicinity of Boston Common, of H. C. (*sic*) Mencken, editor of the *American Mercury*." The Boston *Herald*, still eager to serve Chase's game, sought to make it appear that Wilson's chief objection was to what it called "publicity stunts," and this view was picked up by the press associations, but all the Boston wowsers were well aware that the order meant a radical curtailing of their activities, hitherto so enterprising and carefree, and they were accordingly greatly disturbed. Wilson, in fact was now definitely arrayed against them, and everyone in Boston knew it. "Federal officers," said the Boston *Telegram* on April 23, "want nothing of them. State police have long since refused to aid them in their raids. Boston police, only two days ago, were told by Commissioner Wilson to ignore them. Why? Because it has been shown that Chase, self-styled purist and idealist, is a faker."

On April 20, John J. Mullen, Knopf's chief salesman, called at the Old Corner Bookstore in Boston in the regular course of his business, and was there informed by one Dragon, an officer of the firm, that its head, Richard F. Fuller, was very eager to see him. This was the Fuller we have encountered before. He was the chairman of the Boston Booksellers' Committee, and had long played the sedulous stooge to Chase. At the time of my arrest, as I have noted, he indulged in a great deal of tall talk against me, and offered bets at long odds that I'd be convicted. But now, it appeared, his spirit was chastened, for when he came in presently and took Mullen into his private office, he proposed that we settle the case by accepting a public apology from Chase, and offered to see that it was forthcoming. Here are Mullen's notes of his discourse, sent to Mrs. Knopf in New York that night (Alfred Knopf was transiently out of town):

Talk must be confidential. "Chase is licked—bungled the job—made a damned fool of himself—now you've got nothing to lose by letting him down—damages you'll *not* get— you might get a verdict of $1—long court proceedings, etc., etc. I don't know that I can get Chase to agree to this—but what would you think if I arranged with Chase to make a public apology? Mencken could graciously accept—would have the game and the candle—headlines all over the country. If I can put this over I will make Chase do my bidding— heretofore he has been out of hand."

Mullen was naturally somewhat astonished—and more than a little suspicious. He knew Fuller too well to trust him.

I said to him: "Are you authorized to speak for Chase?" Well, no he was not—"but you know damned well that if I didn't think I could put it over I would not spring the idea." I told Fuller I could not answer for you and Mencken, and that I doubted either of you could give him an answer offhand, for you were in the hands of your lawyers. "Yes, but how would you feel if you had the last word?" I told Fuller that if I had business that was likely to be harassed periodically by such a set I would want to be damned certain that I was properly protected, and would take any and every precaution. "Well," said Fuller, "I know Alfred to be reasonable—when I took up 'Hunger' with him he was most reasonable." I allowed that this was true, and suggested that Fuller should find out first how far he could go, then go to New York and meet you by prearrangement, allowing time for Mencken to get there, and then present his proposition. This he said he would do.

Before I left the store Fuller told me that he had been in touch with Chase, and that they were to meet at 2 P.M. "How can I get in touch with you?" I told him that I had an appointment for 11 A.M. Wednesday [the next day] with Dragon.

Knopf returned to New York the next day, April 21, and, on reading Mullen's report, called me up in Baltimore. Mullen, as his notes show, believed that we should see Fuller, but Knopf was doubtful about it, and so was I. On the same day Mullen met Fuller again. From his notes:

> Chase has been in—they conferred—Fuller "talked to him like a Dutch uncle." Chase is now going to confer with the Rev. Mr. Calkins, president of the Watch and Ward Society, and with Whitman, their lawyer, and will see Fuller again next Monday April 26. Fuller is going away tomorrow for the rest of the week. If Chase *et al* agree to his plan to act as "mediator," he says he will telephone to you (get that telephone—I suggested writing) for an appointment. Fuller says that perhaps it is best not to write to you yet.

On receipt of Mullen's second report, Knopf told him warily that if Fuller happened to be in New York the next Tuesday, April 27, he might drop into the Knopf office, and that I'd possibly be there. Fuller, on being informed of this, proposed Wednesday or Thursday instead, but there the negotiations ended. Mullen was very eager for us to agree to a conference. He believed that Fuller's appearance before us would be sufficient confession that Chase had made a serious blunder in raiding the *American Mercury,* and was well aware of it, and that it didn't make much difference what arrangement was actually reached. He was convinced that Fuller thought Chase was in a difficult and dangerous position, and that he (Fuller) aspired to give him a push downhill, and so augment the independence and power of the Boston Booksellers' Committee. But we distrusted Fuller too much to enter upon parleys with him in the absence of a definite proposal in writing, and in the end we decided not to see him at all. I never laid eyes on him, in fact, until a couple of years later, when Alfred Knopf and I were in

Boston together on business not related to the *American Mercury* case. He was then excessively polite, but my encounter with him was very brief. Hays took no part in this Mullen-Fuller-Chase parley. The question whether we should give any confidence to Fuller was one that Knopf was best fitted to answer, and he disposed of it without legal advice.

As I have recorded, the Cambridge newsdealer, Felix Caragianes, had been found guilty on April 11 by Judge Arthur P. Stone in the District Court at Cambridge, and fined $100, the minimum penalty under the Massachusetts law for vending obscene literature. We had appealed at once in Caragianes's name, and the case was now set down for trial in the Superior Court, Middlesex County, Criminal Division. In the proceedings before Judge Stone, Hays had had the aid of two Cambridge lawyers, Allen E. Throop and Samuel Becker, who were supposed to be experts in the local procedure, but they turned out to be useless, and were not employed subsequently. When Hays began examining the papers on appeal he found that the information against Caragianes did not mention the *American Mercury* at all: it embodied only a general charge that he had sold an "indecent magazine." This fact, he believed, opened a way for attacking the whole proceedings, and he so wrote to Ehrmann. His argument, set forth at length in a letter dated May 14, is worth quoting:

> If the bookseller was charged with having sold an indecent magazine, to wit, the *American Mercury*, by reason of the fact that it contained the article "Hatrack," one could move to dismiss on the ground that that did not constitute a crime, since "Hatrack" was not obscene. Where, however, the information is silent on the specific article and merely charges one with selling indecent magazines, not only is one in a position where one could not prepare for trial,

but one is also in a position where one cannot make a motion to dismiss. Of course, the answer is always made that one knows what the charge is or that a bill of particulars might be asked for, but an information or indictment is decided on the proposition that it contains all the required information and that a man is not assumed to know anything outside of that information.

Bills of particulars may cure details or they may be required to particularize matter that is generally alleged, but I have never understood that they could, in themselves, be regarded as charging the crime. One might just as well say that the State could charge an individual with committing a crime, not even specifying the crime, and then leave him to a bill of particulars to discover what the charge was. But you will note my point here is a little different. If the crime is properly alleged, one can always test on the information or indictment itself whether facts actually constitute a crime. In other words, the information or indictment is itself subject to dismissal.

It has occurred to me that if the judge denies this motion, it might be well to appeal. If, for some procedural reason, that cannot be done, it might be well to ask for a bill of particulars, and then, when they have specified "Hatrack," to move to dismiss and, if we are beaten, carry that up on appeal. Thus we would not have to try the case unless we lose all along the line.

But Ehrmann decided that it would be better to proceed in the more usual manner, and accordingly filed a motion to quash the information. This was before a Judge Gray, then sitting in the Superior Court. Gray refused the motion, but was friendly, and the district attorney, who was also friendly, agreed that if Caragianes would file a plea of *nolo contendere* he (the district attorney) would dispose of the case by "filing the papers," *i.e.,* by letting it drop. He told Hays that, if he had been consulted, Caragianes would never have been arrested. Hays, at the start, was in doubt about

this arrangement. "From a practical point of view," he wrote
to me on May 13, "it might be wise, but psychologically
I am against it. I think we shall win out, and it would be
a mistake to accept any favors." But when he began to reflect
that Caragianes, if convicted, might refuse to appeal, he was
won over, and all hands agreed to the district attorney's plan.
The hearing was eventually set for June 7. Hays, by that
time, was on the way to Europe, and Ehrmann, believing
that only a formality remained, did not go to Cambridge,
but left the matter to Caragianes's own lawyers, Culolias
and Haines, of Boston. When the case was called, however,
there was another judge on the bench, George Flynn by
name, and he turned out to be very hostile. He refused flatly
to countenance the arrangement agreed to by the district
attorney, and ordered the trial of Caragianes to begin at
once. Culolias, after some difficulty, got a postponement
of two days, and on June 9 Ehrmann saw the judge in cham-
bers. Ehrmann first tried to induce him to accept the agreement, and then to postpone the trial until Hays could get
back from Europe, and Asbury and I could be brought to
Cambridge as witnesses. The judge, however, refused to
budge, and Ehrmann thereupon withdrew his appearance
in the case, and that of Hays. This threw poor Caragianes
back upon his own lawyers. They gathered from the fulminations of the judge that if their client pleaded not guilty
and were found guilty he would be given a jail sentence,
so they advised him to plead guilty and have done. This
he did, and Judge Flynn let his fine of $100 stand. We, of
course, paid it.

The day after these proceedings the Associated Press reported from Ottawa that a Canadian member of Parliament
named H. C. Hocken, sitting in the Dominion House of
Commons for the Toronto West Center district, had demanded that the *American Mercury* be excluded from
Canada. It quickly appeared that what the hon. gentleman

objected to was not "Hatrack," but an editorial in the June issue. This editorial, which I had myself written, gave a derisive account of the intellectual and spiritual decay of England, then engaged in a last feverish attempt to drag the United States into the League of Nations. The Hon. Mr. Hocken read a paragraph from it to the House, and inquired of the Government if such sinful stuff would be permitted to circulate in Canada. The Prime Minister, the Right Hon. W. L. Mackenzie King, answering for the Minister of Customs, the Hon. George Boivin, replied that the matter would be looked into at once, and the next day the Canadian papers announced that it was in the hands of Sydney Roe, chief censor of customs. When news of this reached New York I gave the newspapers the following statement:

Section 11, Item 1201, Schedule 6, of the Canadian Tariff Act of 1907 permits the Minister of Customs, in his discretion, to bar from the Dominion magazines of "a treasonable or seditious, or of an immoral and indecent character." Inasmuch as there is no allegation that the editorial in the June issue of the *American Mercury,* on the present low state of English politics, was "immoral or indecent," I assume that it offended as "treasonable or seditious." I can only say that the *American Mercury* acknowledges no allegiance to King George V, and that it is interested in definitions of treason framed by Canadian politicians only as it is interested in other amusing imbecilities. Barring American magazines from the mails is a favorite vote-catching device of these politicians, and at the present moment they have a hundred or more on their list, including many obviously harmless farm papers. Their aim, it appears, is to foster a native magazine industry in Canada, which languishes for reasons set forth by a Canadian journalist, Mr. Fred Jacoob, in the same June number of the *American Mercury.* The last magazine to be barred was *Liberty.* I need not add, I hope, that the *American Mercury* will not permit such puerile and disingenuous attacks to influence its editorial policy in the slightest. It has no desire to be esteemed by Canadian Dogberrys.

The Canadian papers replied with blistering denunciations of the *American Mercury*—the Toronto *Globe*, for example, declaring piously that its constituents were only "the ignorant, the vicious and the uninformed." The *Globe* went on: "We have many individuals of the Mencken type in our own cities. We find them loafing on the street corners, lounging in alleys, huddling in dives." Alfred Knopf and I fully expected that the magazine would be barred from Canada, and on that theory we looked into the feasibility of getting it to subscribers there in sealed envelopes, each containing one or two signatures. Our Canadian circulation was small, both relatively and absolutely, but we were determined to resist losing it. For some reason, however, that never appeared, nothing more was heard of the matter, and though the *American Mercury* was attacked by Canadian politicians and newspapers on various later occasions, it was never actually barred from the Dominion. But these onslaughts always brought us unpleasant notice in the American press, and inspired wowsers to activity, so we watched them carefully.

On receipt of Mullen's reports of his palavers with Fuller I was convinced that the Boston comstocks had begun to fear that they had made a serious blunder, and that it would thus be prudent to push our advantage home by suing them for damages. To be sure, a claim for damages was already attached to our proceedings before Judge Morton in the Federal Court at Boston, but it was somewhat vague, and there were serious technical difficulties in the way of pressing it. As I have recorded, I had deliberately talked of libel suits while I was in Boston, hoping that the news would reach Chase and shake him up, and I had plenty of reason for believing that he was duly shaken. I now concluded that the time had come for action, and urged it upon Hays. I told him that I was especially eager to bring suits not only against Chase, but also against the officers and directors of the Watch and Ward Society, including Charles W. Eliot. Eliot was a vice-president of the organization, and had lent his great name to its nefarious operations. It seemed to me that we'd be doing a public service if we brought home to men of his type their responsibility in such matters. The wowsers everywhere used them as false-faces, taking full advantage of their reputation for integrity, and persons under wowserian attack suffered grave damage in consequence. Once it became known that they could be brought to book they would be more careful, and the wowsers would lose their support. In most cases, perhaps, it was only formal, but nevertheless it was there, and without it the wowsers would be much less dangerous.

Unfortunately, there were some legal obstacles to suing either Chase and his associates personally, or the society as a corporation. The difficulty in the first case was that I had gone to Boston voluntarily, and forced Chase to order my arrest. Thus I could hardly allege that he was the prime mover in it, and my claim for damages began to become somewhat thin. If he had proceeded against me without my consent my acquittal would have laid him open clearly to a suit for false arrest, but all the consent was on my side, and he had, in fact, made diligent efforts to avoid meeting me at all. The *American Mercury*, of course, was in a better position, for it had certainly not consented to the arrest of Caragianes or to his subsequent fulminations in the newspapers, but the *American Mercury* was a corporation, and a corporation, having no soul, could only recover actual damages. It would be very difficult to prove them. As a result of the uproar, to be sure, a few subscribers had cancelled their subscriptions, but they were only a few, and against them stood the thousands who had tried in vain to buy the April issue. On the advertising side the damage suffered was more material, but most of it was not susceptible to proof. Bachman, our advertising manager, prepared a list of advertisements that, in his judgment, had been cancelled or otherwise lost as a result of Chase's attack on the magazine, but it was made up mainly of surmises, and in large part it consisted only of an advertising manager's excuses for not getting business. It would be next to impossible to find an advertiser willing to say under oath that he had kept out of the magazine because Chase had injured its good repute. It would be easier for Chase himself to find one willing to say that he had kept out because he regarded "Hatrack" as indecent.

The second difficulty confronting us had to do with the fact that the Watch and Ward Society was, in the eyes of the Massachusetts law, a charitable trust. The most familiar example of a charitable trust is a hospital. Ordinarily, it cannot be sued for damages, for the law assumes that its funds are devoted to the uses of the indigent sick, and that if it were mulcted in damages these innocents would suffer. In case the wrong eye of a patient is taken out, or the wrong leg cut off, he may sue the surgeons responsible, but he may not sue the hospital. The organizers of the Watch and Ward Society had been smart enough to draw up a charter bringing it under the charitable trust rule, and in consequence its endowment and other funds looked to be beyond the reach of our writ. But I suggested to Hays that it might be possible to challenge, as a matter of fact, its character as a charitable trust, and thus get it into court. I drew up a series of propositions to that effect, and sent them to Hays, and meanwhile he made an investigation of the situation himself, and consulted Ehrmann. Ehrmann was dubious, but Hays was at first hopeful of finding a way. By May 4, however, he had begun to harbor such doubts that he decided not to proceed, and so informed me by letter. But by May 24 he had reached the conclusion that suits might actually lie, and therefore instructed Ehrmann to enter one against Chase. Ehrmann was still unconvinced, and in the end nothing was done. The Knopfs, Alfred and his father Samuel, were not eager for the programme I advocated. The proceedings already under way were costing us a great deal of money, and they were beginning to be a bit war-weary. Alfred was somewhat upset, too, by the fact that Hays also represented Horace Liveright, a rival publisher, and proposed to enter suit against Chase in his name under cover of the Morton decision. Liveright was of bad repute and Knopf detested him. I appealed to Hays to let the Liveright case lie until our own was disposed of, and he agreed to do so, but Liveright was grabbing what publicity he could out of the situation, and so Knopf continued uneasy.

I have always regretted that we didn't sue both Chase and Calkins, the president of the Watch and Ward Society, even though the chance of getting substantial verdicts, or indeed any verdicts at all, was small. Calkins played into our hands on May 4 by giving an interview to the Quincy (Ill.) *Herald* that was full of matter valuable to us. In it he admitted categorically that "Hatrack" was not obscene. "It is," he said, "not sexually exciting, but it is so brutal in its realism as to amount to indecency." For some reason that I forget—probably the fact that I was swamped, in those days, by newspaper clippings—I did not see this interview until July 5, two months afterward. I then wrote to Calkins, asking if he had been reported correctly. He replied on July 8 from Rockport, Mass., saying that he was sending for a copy of the Quincy *Herald,* and would answer when he received it. On July 14 he finally admitted that the report was "in substance . . . probably as accurate as are most reports of interviews not subsequently revised," and a little while later he sent me a formal letter on the stationery of the Watch and Ward Society, repeating this admission. But by that time

Hays was in Europe, and the plan of suing Chase, Calkins, *et al* had receeded into the shadows.

In the meantime, Knopf was preparing to publish "Up From Methodism," the book by Herbert Asbury from which "Hatrack" had come. The story was an essential part of Asbury's narrative, and Knopf proposed to include it, save for a few minor changes, precisely as it had appeared in the *American Mercury*. On August 10 Mullen arrived in Boston with a publisher's dummy on the book, and visited Fuller in the regular course of business. A publisher's dummy consists of the binding, the title page and a few pages of text: the rest is blank. Fuller demanded to know if "Hatrack" were included, and when informed that it was not, asked somewhat indignantly why Mullen was not provided with proof-sheets of it, so that he (Fuller) might read it. There ensued a long and raucous discussion, reported in full by Mullen that night. Mullen insisted that there was no reason why Fuller or anyone else should pass upon the text of "Up From Methodism"—that "Hatrack" had been declared not obscene by a Boston judge, and that no other part of the book had ever been in question. But Fuller, still upset by the failure of his effort to draw us into a treaty of peace with Chase, declared that he had a duty to perform as chairman of the Boston Booksellers' Committee, and that a principal part of that duty, now that the Watch and Ward Society was in a state of innocuous desuetude, was to read suspected books, and warn his fellow booksellers against those likely to be raided by the police. To this Mullen replied that the police had shown no sign of being interested in "Hatrack," and that if they made any attempt on it they would be restrained by the same judicial opinions (Judge Parmenter's and Judge Morton's) that had floored the comstocks. But Fuller kept on insisting that he should have a complete advance copy of the book before Mullen solicited any orders for it in Boston, and Mullen refused to agree.

Mullen had a vast contempt for Fuller, and their palaver was full of animosity on both sides. When Mullen's report reached New York the elder Knopf, Samuel, who was a very excitable man, was consumed by wrath. He denounced Fuller as a hypocrite and a scoundrel, talked of going to Boston to flout him in person, and declared that "Up From Methodism" would be sold there if it was the last Knopf book ever sent to New England. Soon after it was published, which was on September 27, Samuel Knopf actually went to Boston with Hays, and the two of them, along with Ehrmann, met the Watch and Ward Society's lawyer, Whitman, and had what seems to have been an amicable session with him. The book was never challenged, either in Boston or elsewhere. Fuller subsided, and the society had no stomach for another battle. The total sales were 4060 copies for the whole country—a very modest mark, considering the advertising that the book had got.

XI

WHEN Hays and Ehrmann met Whitman they found him eager to get rid of the litigation still pending before Judge Morton. The injunction issued against the Watch and Ward Society was still in effect, and even if we did not proceed further it would remain in effect indefinitely, but there had been no trial of our claim for damages, and the wowsers feared that we might bring it up at any minute. The chances were, as I have explained, that we could not recover anything, but nevertheless the wowsers were very uneasy, and they were uneasy, too, about the possibility of damage suits in the State courts—not only by us, but also by other publishers eager to take rides on our backs. By this time the Watch and Ward Society was trying to evade responsibility by throwing all the blame on poor Chase, who was in a very low state of mind. On October 18 Ehrmann received a letter from Whitman saying that he had been in conference with the officers of the Watch and Ward Society, with Fuller and with Fuller's counsel, and that he was authorized to make the following proposal:

So far as "Up From Methodism" is concerned, in view

of the fact that two judges in Massachusetts have differed in opinion, it does not seem advisable for the society to make any further application to the courts on the "Hatrack" article. As to the pending case, the injunction was limited to threats and intimidation, and I think you will agree that if it had not been for the unfortunate letter of Mr. Chase, the injunction would not have been issued. The form of this letter was unauthorized, and has been discontinued.

After our interview Mr. Knopf, Sr., seemed to agree that some sort of censorship committee was desirable in any community, if fair-minded, inasmuch as the booksellers and magazine distributors cannot be expected to read every book in the rush of business. We would, therefore, make this suggestion: that we have a further conference with you, Mr. Hays and, if he wishes, Mr. Knopf or Mr. Mencken, and go over the constitution and plan of the several committees and the manner in which they have functioned during the years they have been in existence. The Society has no wish to be unfair or unjust to anyone, and is acting in the interest of the public morals. We should welcome your suggestions and criticisms, and I, personally, feel that you will be convinced that at no time has there been any personal animosity against either Mr. Knopf or Mr. Mencken, and that your coöperation is really desired.

Mr. Knopf can rest assured that should he and the Society or the various committees hereafter differ in opinion whether any of his publications violate the statute law of Massachusetts, he will be given an opportunity to test the question in Court, so that he may not feel that he is prevented therefrom by any secret pressure which interferes with the sale of the accused publication. Of course I do not mean to intimate in the slightest that Mr. Knopf is any less interested in the protection of the public morals than anyone here, but in these days of "modern" literature opinions as to the effect of the Massachusetts statute thereon may differ.

If this is agreeable to you, and I understood at our con-

ference that it would be, we can then arrange our litigation by dismissing the bill, and, if you wish it, a stipulation to the effect I have just stated. If Mr. Knopf cares to
consider this suggestion, we should be very glad to take it
up either with you or Mr. Hays, or at the larger conference
I have suggested, at your convenience.

Here was a change of tune, indeed! All the old defiance
was gone, and the wowsers were willing to agree (*a*) to let
"Up From Methodism" go, and "Hatrack" with it, (*b*) to
send out no more intimidating letters to the news companies, (*c*) to question no Knopf book save in open court,
with Knopf getting plenty of notice and a chance to employ
counsel, and (*d*) to sign a stipulation giving permanent effect
to (*c*). Ehrmann forwarded Whitman's letter to Hays on
October 20 with a covering letter suggesting that the
wowsers' offer regarding Knopf books should be extended
to the *American Mercury,* and that we should refuse to take
part in any conference regarding censorship committees,
or to give them any countenance otherwise. Hays was naturally delighted to receive the peace proposals, and in general approved their terms—with, of course, Ehrmann's
amendments. The thing the Watch and Ward Society was
now offering was precisely what we had been fighting for
all the while. I had gone to Boston to challenge Chase's system of suppressing magazines by threat and intimidation,
and to force him to meet me in open court, and now we
had a categorical acknowledgment that I had been right,
and Chase wrong. But though all this was very gratifying,
Hays was disinclined to consent to the vacating of the
Morgan injunction. So long as it was in effect we had a club
to flourish over the wowsers' heads; the moment it was
vacated they might begin to rat on their agreement. No
rational man would or could trust to their honor. The most
we should agree to, Hays believed, was to let our claim for
damages "remain dormant until, in the course of time, it

THE "HATRACK" CASE

is taken off the calendar." The whole question was submitted to the Knopfs and me, and we debated its pros and cons for a week or so. We were all eager, of course, to get rid of the case as soon as possible, for it was consuming a lot of our time and costing a great deal of money, but, with the wowsers plainly on the ropes, we resolved to proceed cautiously, making no concessions that were not absolutely necessary in fairness, and keeping the threat of damage suits in the air until an agreement satisfactory to us was reached.

In the midst of these delays Chase fell ill, and we received news that worry over the case was to blame. He was a sturdy buck, and had been the picture of health when I met him in April, but the battles of the months following had worn him out. Two things, in particular, had consumed his Christian optimism and undermined his vigor. One was the threat, so long hanging over him, that I might sue him personally for damages, and so get my hooks on the house that he had bought out of his hard-earned savings. The other was the fact that his associates in the Watch and Ward Society, wowser-like, had shouldered on him all the blame for their troubles. They knew very well that he was sending out, almost every day, such letters as the one that brought me to Boston, and they had never raised the slightest objection to the fact. On the contrary, Calkins, their president, had publicly approved the practise. But now, as Whitman's letter to Ehrmann shows, they were arguing that the letter that Chase sent to Tracey in the "Hatrack" case was "unfortunate" and "unauthorized." Wowsers always desert one another in times of stress, as my experience in Baltimore had long ago taught me, and when they begin to quarrel their fighting technic is extraordinarily foul. Poor Chase felt that he was now the goat, and feared that he might lose not only his house but also his job.

Winged Mercury was stopped in
    flight,
  We speak of him who did it;
He made the chase, but lost the
    fight,
    His name? Find where we've
        hid it!
And we'll be frank enough to say
His first initial is a J.

J. Frank Chase was featured in the Boston *Post*'s "Picture Rhymes" of "Famous Folks in Week's News" following the encounter with Mencken.

When he took to his bed I don't know, but it was soon after the conference described in Whitman's letter of October 18, from which he had been apparently excluded. The first reports were to the effect that he was not seriously ill, but simply needed a rest. On October 25, however, news came that pulmonary complications had developed, and on November 3 he died. "He had been ill a week of pneumonia," reported the Associated Press, "and had suffered a shock which caused a relapse." The nature of that shock was not disclosed, but we could at least indulge in surmise. I must add this his death did not greatly surprise me. Like all agnostics, I am somewhat superstitious, and one of my superstitions is to the effect that men who set out to do me evil not infrequently die suddenly. I could compile a long list of examples, but this is not the place for it. Chase's death gave me no noticeable grief. He belonged to a type of cleric that is extraordinarily obnoxious to me. I had spent years denouncing others of his kind, and when I met him in Boston I found nothing in him to ameliorate my views of the species. He was a Pecksniff, and, despite all his burly geniality, he looked and acted the part. Boston was full of reports that, like Anthony Comstock, he was extremely fond of the dirty literature he professed to hold in such holy horror, and was in the habit of exhibiting it clandestinely to his friends. A newspaper woman, Katherine Donovan, of the Boston *Advertiser,* informed me that he had once composed an obscene ode to the night clubs of Boston, and read it to a committee of the State Legislature. He told several Boston reporters, who told me, that on one of his frequent visits to New York, he had lain awake all night in a Fall River boat, reading a pornographic novel and experiencing a continuous engorgement of the *corpora cavernosa.* Now he was dead at last in defeat and dismay, and we were rid of him.

Unfortunately, his death rather heartened his fellow-wowsers of the Watch and Ward Society. Since he was now silent, at least until the Resurrection Day, they were free to blame everything on him, and he could no longer blame anything on them. Moreover, they were quick to see that we were handicapped by the fact that we could never again bring him into court. "The situation," wrote Whitman to Ehrmann on November 5, "is changed by the death of Mr. Chase"—and thereafter Whitman's letters were appreciably less conciliatory. On December 11 he wrote to Ehrmann reiterating the society's pledge "not to do anything to interfere with the sale of 'Up From Methodism' in Boston" and renewing its promise to proceed against no Knopf book thereafter, and no issue of the *American Mercury* save by "testing the question in court," but to the latter stipulation he now added a disingenuous qualification. I quote:

> It is not, and will not be, the policy of the society to prevent by threat or intimidation the circulation of publications which it believes offend the statute; but the society cannot commit itself to a policy whereby it cannot communicate by letter or otherwise its opinion as to such publications *to law-enforcing agencies and others interested in securing the opinion of the society.* What we do say is that so far as the magazine is concerned we will notify you that we intend to proceed, either directly or by presenting the matter to the district attorney. So far as books are concerned, I understand that the practise in the past has been that when the Booksellers' Committee, after conference with the Watch and Ward Society, has come to the conclusion that a book offends the Massachusetts statute, the publisher is notified to that effect. *This practise will be continued so far as we are able to effect it.*

The italics are mine. Whitman was hiding behind the exact terms of Judge Morton's injunction, and likewise behind the death of Chase. Morton had forbidden the wowsers to interfere "with the sale and distribution of any future issues of the *American Mercury* by organized threat and intimidation, whether direct or covert," and Whitman was now trying to make it appear that this had never been the policy of the Watch and Ward Society—that what Judge Morton had forbidden was the unauthorized act of Chase alone. As for the "law-enforcement agencies" mentioned in his letter, it was apparent from the text that the Boston Booksellers' Committee was included, and it was also apparent that he was trying to get in the Massachusetts Magazine Committee, too. What his promise to proceed only by open trial in open court amounted to was made manifest by the next paragraph of his letter:

> You, as a Massachusetts lawyer, do not need to be informed of the extreme sensitiveness of the authorities of the Catholic Church to any printed matter which, in their opinion, is injurious to sexual morality, and inasmuch as the officers of the law in Suffolk county, including quite a majority of the jurymen, are communicants of that church, all that is really necessary for the Watch and Ward Society to do is to refer a publication, which in their opinion offends the Massachusetts statute, to the duly constituted authorities, and, of course, we reserve the entire right to adopt and continue that practise.

Certainly this was plain enough. In brief, we could let the society go on favoring the Boston Booksellers' Committee and the Massachusetts Magazine Committee with orders disguised as advice, Morton injunction or no injunction, or we could take our chances with the Irish Catholic judges, district attorneys and juries of the Boston area. There would be no more hearings before Unitarian Judge Parmenters. The next case would be steered to a Catholic municipal judge, and by him it would be swiftly sent to a Catholic Superior Court judge and jury, with a Catholic district attorney prosecuting. "We trust this frank statement," continued Whitman with some humor, "will meet your views. We again reiterate that, in spite of Mr. Mencken's suspicions, there has been at no time any personal animus against either him or his publication, and no discriminations have been attempted or intended between magazine publishers." Finally, Whitman let it be known delicately that what he expected for his now-so-greatly modified concessions was the dismissal of the claim for damages under the Morton injunction, and the vacating of the injunction itself. It was a thorn in the carcass of the Watch and Ward Society, not only because of its direct effect but also because it had inspired other publishers to resist the society's methods. One of these publishers was the company issuing *Snappy Stories,* a frankly bawdy magazine, often banned in Boston and elsewhere. So long as the *Snappy Stories* case was pending, concluded Whitman, he would not ask us to move for the dismissal of our own case, "but very likely Mr. Hays will feel that after this whole matter has blown away it is just as well to voluntarily clear the court docket rather than wait for a tardy dismissal by the court."

Ehrmann referred this letter to Hays, and Hays sent it to us. We refused to accept the terms it offered, and Hays wrote to Ehrmann instructing him to so inform Whitman. I quote:

> We do not object to any society giving its opinion to law-enforcing agencies; we *do* object to their giving an opinion to booksellers which is interpreted by the booksellers as a threat or a bluff, and which opinion they follow *whether or not* the book or magazine violates the law. If the opinion is either given to us or to any law-enforcing agency we can have no objection. But if the idea is to notify booksellers, then such action would seem to be directly contrary to the law as laid down by Judge Morton in the *American Mercury* case. I do not suppose that Mr. Whitman intends this.

The italics are mine.

But that, of course, was precisely what Whitman did intend. His idea was to get rid of Judge Morton's prohibition of "organized threat and intimidation" by blaming it all on poor Chase, now dead and in Heaven—and then to resume the same thing under another and more mellifluous name. On November 26 he wrote to Ehrmann again. Here are the essential parts of his letter:

> I think you are fighting a windmill because you are classifying yourself with such filth as *Snappy Stories* has produced in the past. It is quite evident that the news distributors do not have the time to read every magazine that comes into their hands before distribution, and there has been a magazine as well as a book committee composed of publishers and distributors to act in conference with the Watch and Ward Society. You apparently assume that the distributors are anxious and willing to circulate obscene literature. They, however, are just as anxious as anyone else to protect the public from such publications, and you may be well assured that the Watch and Ward Society will not threaten anybody about your publications, and, on the other hand, they can not give up the right to call to the attention of the magazine distributors' committee their views of any publication which they deem offending. You are wholly in error in thinking that the distributors stand in terror of the Watch and Ward Society. On the contrary they have at all times welcomed its coöperation and in case of doubt have submitted to their own counsel publications which have met the criticism of the society.

In conclusion, Whitman suggested that Knopf or I come to Boston for a conference "with the various committees, so that they may thoroughly understand what is being done." But we knew only too well what was being done, and accordingly refused. On November 27 Hays wrote to Ehrmann:

Mr. Mencken and Mr. Knopf have no desire to go to Boston to confer with any committees; they merely have a desire to do their business in a legitimate manner. There is only one thing that we ask of Mr. Whitman and the Watch and Ward Society, and that is that if there is any complaint by them or anyone else in Boston against any books published by Knopf, a charge be made in a court of law against somebody instead of their suggesting to people associated with them that it is dangerous to buy goods from us. The issue is perfectly clear. We are not asking for very much. When we went into court on this occasion, the court held that we had a right to be free from action which may be interpreted by booksellers either as a threat or a bluff, for it is always one or the other. The law having been established in one case, we see no reason why we should be compelled to go to the expense in the future of proceeding in the same way. These people know we are not in the business of publishing pornographic books, and all we ask in case of any difference of opinion is for our day in court.

If they will give us their assurance that we will have this if the occasion arises in the future, then we have no desire for damages. If, however, we cannot get this assurance, we might just as well go ahead with this case and make it clear that where our rights are violated, somebody will have to pay damages.

On December 2 Hays wrote to Ehrmann again, suggesting that if Whitman, as counsel to the Watch and Ward Society, were willing to promise categorically and in writing that it would no longer intimidate newsdealers by threats we'd agree, despite our continuing doubts of his *bona fides,* to accept it at its face value, and so bring what had begun to seem a vain correspondence to an end. He enclosed a draft of the letter he had in mind, as follows:

In reference to the *American Mercury* case and the publications of your company, my clients, the Watch and Ward Society, are ready to take the position that if we have any complaint at any time against the *Mercury* or any of your publications, we shall notify you. We do not intend, directly or indirectly, to advise or warn your customers, but in the event that in our view any book or any part of the *Mercury* is in violation of the law of Massachusetts and we wish to test the question, we shall take proper legal proceedings against any individual concerned.

Ehrmann saw Whitman on December 9, and they discussed the business at length. The *Snappy Stories* case, by this time, was worrying the Watch and Ward Society, and impeding our own negotiations. Whitman feared that if *Snappy Stories* obtained an injunction similar to ours, the way would be open for flooding Boston with frankly indecent magazines. He was therefore reluctant to sign the stipulation that Hays had drawn up. He argued that its provisions would probably have to be extended, soon or late, to other magazines, and that if that were done a magazine full of "lewd and lascivious matter" might be distributed and sold in Boston before the publisher could be notified and brought into court. This, of course, was a real enough difficulty. Many such magazines were published by racketeers of no responsibility. They would welcome the chance to sell their product and run. It would be hard, in most cases, to get them into court, and the worst of them would not be stopped by an occasional fine, nor even by an occasional jail sentence. Whitman accordingly proposed that, as a condition of his signing the stipulation prepared by Hays, we agree to provide the smelling committee of the Watch and Ward Society with advance copies of future issues of the *American Mercury,* so that any which appeared to menace the moral grandeur of Massachusetts might be brought into court for judgment in advance of their actual distribution.

"This suggestion," wrote Ehrmann to Hays, "seems to me worthy of consideration. We gain our point to the extent that the society will not warn or advise distributors; in return, we agree to make a test case by the sale of one copy before distribution. If any of your distributors receive advance copies, the society might refer to such copies so that they might come to a decision quickly as to whether they wish a test case. As a matter of fact, I believe that we are dealing with a question which will probably prove academic so far as the Watch and Ward Society is concerned. Chase is dead, and the society has had one very disagreeable experience and does not desire another."

But though Ehrmann was thus considerably impressed by Whitman's argument, Hays and I were not. We were certainly not going to send advance copies of the *American Mercury* to the Watch and Ward Society or to any other gang of wowsers. It was our whole contention that they had no business to censor what we printed—that their sole legitimate recourse, in case they wanted to risk another battle, was to bring us into court *after* publication and distribution. Accordingly, Hays wrote to Ehrmann as follows on December 10:

> Whitman's proposition is wholly unsatisfactory. He would, no doubt, make the same proposal to anyone. He seems entirely to ignore the fact that in the one case where the issue was tested, the court held the procedure of the society to be illegal. We have asked that they agree not to adopt that procedure again either in connection with the *Mercury* or any other publication of Knopf. The Watch and Ward Society, with admirable nonchalance, simply ignores the court decision. We had better prepare for the trial of the case.

Hays instructed Ehrmann to show Whitman this letter, and it was done. A copy of it was sent to me and another

to Alfred Knopf, and on December 13 Knopf wrote to Hays
as follows:

> It seems to all of us now that there will be little use in
> further dealing with Whitman. It is as clear to us as it is
> to you how outrageous his latest proposal is and we can
> only wonder at the attitude expressed by Ehrmann in his
> letter to you of December 9. It certainly seems to me that
> we should press vigorously to have the injunction made
> permanent and consider seriously what damages we can
> prove. Personally, Ehrmann's suggestion that Whitman's
> suggestion "seems to me worthy of consideration" leaves
> me perfectly aghast.

I wrote to Hays to the same effect, and the fat was in
the fire once more. There was a further exchange of letters
between Ehrmann and Whitman, but it got no further than
mere sauciness, and so came to nothing. On December 14
Whitman wrote to Ehrmann as follows:

> I would remind you that a decree in equity is based on
> the situation at the time the decree is entered and that you
> will face quite a different state of facts from that presented
> at the time of Judge Morton's order, as the Watch and Ward
> Society now is working in entire harmony with the com-
> mittees of publishers and news distributors to avoid the dis-
> tribution of filth in Massachusetts. If your clients desire to
> put themselves into that class, we are ready to meet the case.

To this Ehrmann replied as follows the next day:

> "Entire harmony" is generally, if not necessarily, the key-
> note of every illegal combination. In this respect I do not
> see any material difference in the present situation from
> the plan outlined by you at the preliminary hearing. . . .
> Our clients have not put themselves into any class except
> to join the thin ranks of those who are willing to fight for

fundamentals. Chase and Calkins have done the classifying. Incidentally, your recent suggestion, which I have passed along to Mencken, has not only brought his wrath about my head, but has apparently reminded him of a forgotten assignment at Armageddon.

Ehrmann continued to be doubtful about the success of a claim for damages under the Morton injunction, and so wrote to Hays on December 15. There ensued a considerable correspondence between Ehrmann and Hays, some extracts from which I here borrow. Hays to Ehrmann, January 5, 1927:

> I have just conferred with Mencken and the advertising people in reference to damages in our case. While our evidence will be somewhat sketchy, yet, to some extent, we may be able to prove a case. This is so, not only in connection with advertising, but also in connection with the cancellation of subscriptions. I am enclosing herewith memorandum of advertising contracts which we claim were lost because of the action of the Watch and Ward Society.

The reference here, of course, was to the lists of lost advertisements prepared by Bachman and Brockway, already referred to in this chronicle. They were extremely dubious and going into court with them would involve grave risks. Again, from the same letter:

> Our friend Chase being dead, the question arises as to whether we can use the testimony he gave before. Let me know about this. Also, how does the case come up on the calendar? Do you and Whitman agree to set it for a certain day? I should like to see it reached for trial some time early in March.

To this Ehrmann replied on January 8:

If any of the *Mercury* advertisers will say they cancelled the contract because of the suppression of the magazine by the Watch and Ward Society, we ought to take a few depositions. I feel that the advertisers may not go farther than to state that they were moved by the prosecution and publicity, or by the article itself, rather than by the actions of the Watch and Ward Society. On the other hand, we might be able to convince the judge that the proximate cause of all our trouble was the arbitrary or malicious action of the Watch and Ward Society.

In regard to using Chase's testimony, I believe that it is admissible on three grounds:

1. The testimony was actually given in the same cause of action and in the same court in which further testimony will be taken and which has jurisdiction.

2. Chase was a defendant.

3. He comes under the rule relating to dead witnesses.

I have not made an exhaustive search of the law but this is my strong impression.

I have written to Whitman in regard to a trial date.

Other letters followed, and on January 27 Hays sent me a summary of the situation, to wit:

I have now received the material in connection with proof of damages, with the exception of that relating to subscriptions that were cancelled.

In the whole matter we are on pretty thin ice so far as damages go. There is, of course, no way of proving that any difficulty with advertising arose through the action of the Watch and Ward Society rather than through the article itself. It is a pure inference that the refusal of anyone to advertise had anything to do with the Boston episode. A study of the case emphasizes the difficulty. In a case like this it is clear that we claim special damages which must be alleged and proved. We have not alleged them in our papers (as we could not at the time). We shall have to amend our papers.

An amusing authority on this is the case of *Gott v. Pulsifer*, 122 Mass. 135, where a newspaper published a statement reflecting on the authenticity of the well-known Cardiff Giant. The exhibitor claimed to have lost considerable money by this. Among other prospects, an individual named Palmer had agreed to pay $17,000 for a one-half interest in the Giant and he refused to carry out his agreement, testifying that it was because of this publication. In other words, they had pretty clear proof of damage and it was allowed. In connection therewith, the court said:

"The only ground on which it [the action] can be maintained is special damage, which must be set out in the declaration and established by the proof. The only allegation of special damage is in relation to the transaction with Palmer. To sustain this action the plaintiff must prove and the jury must be satisfied * * * that it occasioned special damage to him, the plaintiff, by reason of the contract with Palmer, which *would have been otherwise carried through.*"

The plaintiff had attempted to prove general damage; in other words, had tried to show that the value of the statue as a scientific curiosity or for exhibition had been lessened, but such claim was eliminated.

I am extremely doubtful of whether we can prove, even to the satisfaction of ourselves, that by reason of the Boston incident we lost advertising contracts which would otherwise have been consummated.

I am, however, advising Ehrmann to amend our papers to allege special damages and this is particularly in the hope that Whitman, not knowing of our difficulties, may sing a different song. Will you, therefore, have the *Mercury* send me a statement of loss in subscriptions so that I can add this to the other matter?

The list of lost subscribers, as I have noted, was much shorter and hardly more persuasive than the list of lost advertising, and Ehrmann continued to be convinced that it would be imprudent to press the claim for damages. "If we do nothing at all about the case," he wrote to Hays on January 29, "it will not be dismissed until January, 1929. Meanwhile, Judge Morton's decision has become embalmed in the Federal Reporters' System, and for our purposes cannot be improved upon. From a realistic point of view I can see nothing to gain by trying the case. If the Watch and Ward Society should interfere with any of Knopf's publications, which seems entirely unlikely in view of Chase's death, the case can be marked for trial within two years. On the other hand, if we try the case, there is always the possibility of a reversal and the difficulty of proving any damages. The loss of advertising business must be traced to threats by the defendants to news distributors, and not to publicity following the arrest of Mencken." Hays sent this letter to me, and I wrote to him on January 31:

> It is too bad, but let us keep on. God may deliver us. . . . Can't we argue that we have been damaged to the extent of the cost of meeting and refuting Chase's false charges?

Apparently we couldn't. On the same day Hays suggested to Ehrmann that we "amend our bill of complaint to allege special damages or file a bill of particulars of special damages," but Ehrmann replied with objections to the plan, and after a couple of weeks of further consideration Hays concluded that he was probably right, and wrote to us as follows:

> After very careful consideration I have come to the conclusion that we cannot succeed in proving damages in the Federal case in Boston. I refer you to my letter of January 27, which sets forth the law. Further investigation has confirmed the opinion therein expressed.
>
> We can show a statement of a considerable loss in advertising which might have been due to the Boston episode. Before sending this statement to Ehrmann, however, it

occurred to me that Whitman, on receipt of it, might write to the various advertisers. He might do this in the thought that it is necessary to prepare himself for trial and that letters to those advertisers might elicit the response that they had not advertised in the *Mercury* for other reasons. I think the chance of Whitman doing this is small, but if he did do it, it might put us in a very embarrassing position.

If we do not proceed further the injunction will remain as it is. Incidentally, you will save from $750 to $1000 in legal fees.

I hesitate to advise this because of the personal inclination, in which I know Mr. Mencken shares, to follow the matter up to the limit. Knowing, however, that we hit the climax at the time the injunction was obtained and feeling that an effort to prove damage might make us appear ridiculous, I think it is a mistake to proceed. Sending our claims for damages to Whitman might work as a bluff, and, on the other hand, it might result in embarrassment to us. Please let me have your views.

In the face of these doubts and dubieties there was nothing for us to do save acquiesce. So that was the end of our battle with the Watch and Ward Society. We got no damages —but the injunction that Judge Morton had given us was still good for two years. Whitman made no effort to appeal it. He had a healthy fear of the judges of the First Federal Circuit, and was anything but eager to appear before them as spokesman for the Watch and Ward Society. On January 31, 1929 the case was finally closed with the receipt by Hays of the following notice:

DISTRICT COURT OF THE UNITED STATES

District of Massachusetts

Office of the Clerk
311 Federal Building
Boston

January 30, 1929.

Arthur Garfield Hays, Esq.,
80 Federal street.,
Boston, Mass.

Dear Sir:

The cases listed below in which you appear as counsel were dismissed on January 2, 1929 without prejudice and without costs for lack of prosecution during the two years preceding under General Order of Court dated September 19, 1922.

Any case so dismissed may for good cause shown be revived and restored to the docket upon motion filed on or before March 1, 1928, [The date here, I assume, should have been 1929.] and after due notice to parties.

Very truly yours,
(Signed) JAMES S. ALLEN, Clerk.

2541 Equity, for *American Mercury,* Inc. v. J. Frank Chase, *et al.*

XII

THERE remained our case against the Postoffice. On May 11, 1926, as I have recounted in Section IX, Judge Julian W. Mack issued a sweeping injunction restraining the Postoffice from refusing to carry our April issue, and on July 1 the Postoffice filed a notice of appeal. The hearing on the appeal got on the calendar of the Circuit Court of Appeals for the Second Circuit in November, but it was not until the Spring of the next year that the case was actually argued. The judges sitting were Martin T. Manton, Learned Hand and Thomas W. Swan. Hays appeared for us, and the Postoffice was represented by Charles H. Tuttle, Federal district attorney at New York and three of his assistants. Hays's main argument was one that he had presented to Judge Mack in the court below—that the Postoffice had attacked us wantonly and without plausible cause, *after* the issue complained of had actually gone through the mails. This seemed to us to be the very foundation of our case. The Postoffice had admittedly achieved no conceivable public good by barring the April issue: it had simply damaged us before the country, and given aid and encouragement to the Boston comstocks. But it was this fact precisely that brought us to defeat in the end, for the Circuit Court of Appeals, taking refuge behind the rule that equity offers a remedy only for continuing injuries, turned us out of court. In other words, the Postoffice was permitted to plead its very offense as a defense! But perhaps I had better give the decision in full. It was written by Judge Manton, and was as follows:

The injunction *pendente lite* was granted below, restraining and enjoining the Postmaster of the City of New York and the Postmaster-General, their agents and employés, pending the trial of this cause, from treating the April, 1926, issue of the appellee's magazine, the *American Mercury*, as non-mailable and directing them to transmit that issue through the mails. Two articles, one entitled "Hatrack" and another "A New View of Sex," and an advertisement by one Henry F. Marks' Book Shop, containing information as to where certain obscene books specifically mentioned in the advertisement might be purchased and the price thereof, caused the Postmaster-General to issue an order holding that this issue was unmailable pursuant to Sec. 211 of the United States Criminal Code and Sec. 470 of the Postal Laws and Regulations of 1924. This order was issued because it was found that the specified matters tended to corrupt the morals of those into whose hands they might fall and further, that it gave information where, how and from whom and by what means obscene, lewd or lascivious and indecent books and publications might be obtained.

The bill alleges that the April number was submitted to the postmaster at Camden, N.J., where the magazine is printed, on March 15, 1926, and no objection was made thereto. That practically the whole of the edition of this issue was mailed and delivered before April 5, 1926. The editor of the magazine submitted an affidavit in support of the application for an injunction and swore that the April issue was published in March, 1926, and, in accordance with its usual practice, submitted to the postmaster of Camden, N.J., where the magazine is printed, before March 15, 1926 and that no objection was made thereto and practically the whole of the edition was mailed and delivered before April 5, 1926. In a notice sent out to the "Friends of the *American Mercury*," he said, after stating that the issue had been submitted to the postmaster at Camden before March 15, 1926, and the number had been passed, "the whole edition had been mailed and delivered before April 5—all save a few copies held for stock. The question of the mailability of the number was thus purely academic." His grievance, as stated in his affidavit, was that "Although practically all of said April number had been distributed, the mere fact that the Postoffice officials have made this order of non-mailability stamps the magazine as an obscene publication and doubts have arisen as to whether the said order refers only to the April number or to the magazine in general. The right to transmit later issues of said magazine through the mails will not restore the confidence to which the complainant is entitled." In an affidavit submitted in opposition, Postmaster Kiely swore that no copy of the April, 1926, issue of the *American Mercury* had been refused the privileges of the mail and there was no copy in the Post-office at New York.

Section 396 of the Revised Statutes imposes the duty on the Postmaster-General to superintend generally the business of the department and execute all laws relative to the postal service. The postal laws and regulations of 1924, Sec. 470, declare as non-mailable matter, every obscene, lewd, or lascivious book, pamphlet, picture, paper, letter, writing, print, or other publication of an indecent character, and every written or printed card, letter, circular, book, pamphlet, advertisement, or notice of any kind giving information, directly or indirectly, where, or how, or from whom, or by what means any of the hereinbefore mentioned matters, articles, or things may be obtained or made. It forbids conveying through the mails or delivering from any postoffice by any letter carrier such prohibited literature, and, for a violation of this statute, a penalty is imposed of fine or imprisonment. Section 474 of the same law requires the Postmaster before giving opinions to the public, to submit the question, with a sample of the proof, to the solicitor for the Postoffice Department for instructions. He, by Sec. 10, paragraph 3, relating to the duties of the Solicitor of the Postoffice Department, is charged with the duty of giving opinions to the Postmaster-General and the heads of the several departments upon questions of law arising upon and construction of the postal laws and regulations or otherwise in the course of the postal service with the consideration of all service relative to the mailability of the alleged indecent and obscene matter. Section 211 of the United States Criminal Code is similar to Sec. 470 of the Postal Laws and Regulations referred to.

We may consider the April, 1926, issue only, for it alone is forbidden the use of the mails. It appears from the above quotations from the pleadings and the affidavit of the editor, that such issue has had full use of the mails. The department made its order of prohibition on April 8, 1926, when, according to the appellee's assertion, the whole issue of this edition was mailed and delivered before April 5, 1926. The postmaster in New York City points out and, indeed, the appellee concedes that every copy mailed was delivered and as the editor says, "the question of mailability of the number was thus purely academic." All that may be argued now is that had additional copies been deposited in the mail by the appellee, the Postoffice Department would have refused to accept them. It is not claimed that such deposit will ever be made. It had not when suit was commenced. Under these facts, the motion for temporary injunction should have been denied. U.S. v. American-Asiatic S.S. Co., 242 U.S. 537; U.S. v. Hamburg-American Co., 239 U.S. 466. An injunction *pendente lite* should be granted only where it is made to appear in the moving papers that the absence of such restraining order will cause irreparable injury during the pendency of the action. Such provisional or preventive remedy is given to preserve the *status quo* and to prevent further perpetration of acts which might materially endanger the complainant. Usually a temporary injunction contemplates relief where, without it, final relief would be of no avail to the complainant. Louisville & N.R. Co. v. Western Union Telegraph Co., 252 F. 29; Love v. Atchison, 185 F. 321; Pomeroy Equity Jurisprudence, Sec. 1685. A rule of law cautions us to proceed with great deliberation where the injunction *pendente lite* will in effect determine the litigation and give the party seeking the relief the entire relief which is prayed for in the final decree. Best Food Inc. v. Hemphill Packing Co., 295 F. 425; Mackay Tel. & Cable Co. v. City of Texarkana, 199 F. 347; Taylor & Co. v. Southern Pac. Co., 122 F. 147. While the Postmaster-General has a duty and the power of determining what is non-mailable (Bates & Guild Co. v. Payne, 194 U.S. 106), and the courts may interfere when he is clearly wrong (School of Magnetic Healing v. McAnnulty, 187 U.S. 94; Masses Pub. Co. v. Patten, 246 F. 24), still, we should not make a judicial determination as to the correctness of his ruling upon papers which fail to support a claim of irreprable damage which might occur before final hearing. Injunctive relief contemplates future injury—not that which has happened. An action at law affords redress for such injuries. The claim of damage or harm to appellee's business is a matter where the remedy at law is adequate and must be pursued. The application for a temporary injunction *pendente lite* was improvidently granted.

  Order reversed.

This was the end of the "Hatrack" case. The injunction against the Watch and Ward Society that Judge Morton had given us in Boston was still good, and we never heard another word from the wowsers there so long as I was editor of the *American Mercury,* but the Postoffice went unscathed for Donnelly's malicious and disingenuous attempt to injure us. To be sure, we were never troubled by him again, but the April issue was still barred from the mails, at least in theory. Rather curiously, the decision of Judges Manton, Hand and Swan got very little attention from the newspapers, and we soon found that most persons had not heard of it. To this day those who remember the case at all appear to believe that we won all along the line. Morally speaking, we undoubtedly did, but in the legal sense we were floored finally by three judges in high esteem as Liberals! It was an ending not without its ironies.

We considered an appeal to the Supreme Court of the United States, but the lawyers decided that it would be difficult, in view of the grounds of the decision, to raise a constitutional question, and that in consequence the court would very likely refuse to grant us *certiorari.* The case, by this time, had cost us nearly $20,000, and we were not eager to put any more money into it. We had paid Hays a fee of $7500, and his expenses ran to $1500 more. Out of his $7500 he had paid Ehrmann, but there were other heavy costs, including that of scrapping and reprinting the issue of the *American Mercury* for May, 1926. Because Hays was also attorney for the American Civil Liberties Union there was an impression at the time that it was aiding us, but it actually gave us no help whatsoever, save to refer to the case, now and then, in its monthly bulletins. We received no material assistance from any other source. A day or two before I went to Boston Paul Patterson, president of the A. S. Abell Company, publishers of the Baltimore *Sunpapers,* and a very good friend, asked me if I needed any money, but I replied that I didn't. As a matter of fact, the *American Mercury* had a surplus of nearly $25,000 in cash when the case began.

In 1934 one Burton Rascoe alleged in print that I had demanded a contribution from Theodore Dreiser on the ground that when his (Dreiser's) book, "The 'Genius,'" fell afoul of the comstocks in New York in 1915, I managed and financed the ensuing battle against them. The inspiration of this nonsense was the fact that Rascoe had asked me to turn over to him my rights to various contributions of mine to the *Smart Set,* in order that he might make a *Smart Set* Anthology, and that I had refused. My refusal was based on the ground that I regarded him as hardly more than a literary racketeer, and had no desire to make him free of my property or to show any public connection with him. It is true that I managed and financed the so-called Dreiser Protest—it cost me $300 for postage and clerical help—, but I had not seen or heard from Dreiser since the day before my mother's death, on December 13, 1925, and not a word came from him during the whole course of the "Hatrack" case. I never heard from him again, indeed, until Rascoe's idiotic story was published, when he wrote to me saying that it was not based, as Rascoe alleged, upon his (Dreiser's) authority, and certifying that I had never made any demand on him whatsoever, whether in 1926 or at any other time. I also had a letter from Groff Conklin, Rascoe's collaborator in "The *Smart Set* Anthology," expressing his regret for the silly lie.

The "Hatrack" case played hob with my book, "Notes on Democracy," published in October, 1926. I had begun it in the Summer of 1925, but work upon it was interrupted by the illness and death of my mother. I resumed the writing in January, 1926, but had hardly got a good pace when the raid on the *American Mercury* took me away from the MS. for months. It was well into June before I returned to work on it, and by that time Knopf was growing impatient, and I had to push the writing. The result was a half-baked book which got and deserved bad notices, and sold less than any other volume I have ever written, save only "Making a President." One of the few readers who appeared to find it meritorious was the former German Kaiser. He wrote to me thanking me for the pleasure he had got out of it, and sent me two autographed photographs of him-

Seattle (Wash.)
Star

MENCKEN WINS MERCURY FIGHT

Postoffice Can't Interfere With Mail Circulation

INJUNCTION GRANTED

Judge Says "Hatrack" Not Indecent, but Disgusting

NEW YORK, May 12—H. L. Mencken, the sage of Baltimore and editor of the American Mercury, won a signal victory in court Tuesday when Federal Judge Julian Mack granted a temporary injunction restraining Postmaster-General New from interfering with the distribution of the April number of the magazine.

The issue had been barred from the mails on the application of citizens of Farmington, Mo., who claimed that an article, "Hatrack," written by Herbert Asbury, who lived there when a boy, was indecent.

The magazine had also been the target of the Watch and Ward society of Boston, who stopped sale of the magazine in Boston and had Mencken arrested for selling a copy on the streets. The editor was subsequently discharged.

Judge Mack ruled that "Hatrack" was not indecent, altho he called it "disgusting."

In opposing the injunction, attorneys for the government contended the opposition was not based on the article alone, but also on advertisements of "objectionable" books. The judge said he did not think a publisher was responsible for the contents of books advertised in his publication.

Lubbock (Tex.)
Avalanche

'Hatrack' Wins In Federal Court

Cleveland (O.) Times

MENCKEN WINS IN COURT

Rochester (N.Y.)
Times Union

U. S. FAILS TO BAR MERCURY FROM MAILS

Federal Judge Holds "Hatrack" "Disgusting" but Not Indecent — Other Counts Dismissed

New Orleans (La.)
Tribune

MAIL BAN ON 'HATRACK' IS HELD UP

Mencken Given Injunction Restraining Interference on Postoffice

"DISGUSTING," NOT "INDECENT," RULE

"Objectionable Books" Advertisements Cited by Opposition

Los Angeles (Calif.)
News

MENCKEN VICTOR AS INJUNCTION GRANTED

self. In the years following I heard from various American visitors to Doorn that he had mentioned it to them, and praised it highly. As soon as the "Hatrack" case was cleared off by the adverse decision of the Second Circuit Court of Appeals I began work on "Treatise on the Gods," which I had had in mind for a long while, and after more than two years of hard writing it was finished at last on Thanksgiving Day, 1929. It was published in March, 1930, and had the largest sale of any of my books until the fourth edition of "The American Language" in 1936.

Baltimore, December, 1937.   H. L. Mencken.

Acknowledgments

Along with the publishing firm of Roberts Rinehart, Inc., I am grateful to the Enoch Pratt Free Library, acting through Ms. Averil Kadis, for permission to publish Mencken's manuscript history of the "Hatrack" case. This permission has been granted under the terms of Mencken's will. Also, I appreciate the many courtesies extended to me by Mr. Neil Jordahl, head of humanities at the Library. At the University of Maryland I am indebted for administrative support to Professor Gordon Kelly, head of the American Studies department, and to Professors Richard Cross and Sherod Cooper, head and acting associate head, respectively, of the English department. For research and secretarial assistance I am indebted to Ms. Melissa Hilbish and Ms. Katie Helene, both in the American Studies department. At Roberts Rinehart, Inc., Frederick Rinehart earned my gratitude for his help. Lastly, I found in John Schwartz an ideal editor, starting with the time when he broached the idea of issuing Mencken's account of the "Hatrack" case.

C.B.